About the Gospel

PREACHER'S HANDBOOK
New Series NUMBER 2

Edited by JOHN STACEY

The Local Preachers' Department
of the Methodist Church

© The Local Preachers' Department
of the Methodist Church, 1971
Printed in Great Britain by
The Garden City Press Limited
Letchworth, Hertfordshire, SG6 IJS

SBN 7162 0194 1

Enquiries should be addressed to
The Distributors
The Methodist Book Room
2 Chester House
Pages Lane
London N10 1PZ

Contributors

John Stacey is Secretary of the Local Preachers' Department of the Methodist Church and author of *John Wyclif and Reform*, *About the Ministry* and *The New Superstition*.

W. David Stacey is a Senior Lecturer at Homerton College, Cambridge, and author of *The Pauline View of Man, Is that Good Doctrine?* and *The Man from Nazareth*.

Robert Way-Rider is a Methodist Minister now serving as Senior Lecturer in Divinity at Chester College of Education with special responsibility for New Testament and Patristics. Since 1951 he has been engaged in research into the Apostolic Preaching and its development in the Early Church.

Robin E. Hutt is Chaplain at Kent College, Canterbury. He was trained at Wesley College, Bristol, and holds the Bristol B.A. in Theology. Previously he was a teacher in Birmingham. He served on the Working Party which produced the new experimental scheme of local preacher training.

Pauline M. Webb is an accredited local preacher who is at present responsible for lay training in the Methodist Church. Formerly Editor of the Methodist Missionary Society, she has travelled widely both in this country and overseas. In 1965 she was elected Vice-President of the Methodist Conference, and at present she holds the office of Vice-Chairman of the Central Committee of the World Council of Churches.

John H. S. Crossley was trained for the ministry at Wesley House, Cambridge, and went to Nigeria in 1954. He now works at the Study Centre for Islam and Christianity in Ibadan.

Eric W. Blennerhassett was a circuit minister for eight years, a producer with the religious broadcasting staff of the B.B.C. in Birmingham for nine, with the Churches' Television Centre at Bushey for four, and is now responsible for the contributions of the churches of all denominations to the programmes of Radio London.

Contents

Contents

Editorial

John Stacey

IT IS PART of my work to travel the land conferring with lay people who are committed to Christian preaching. Not surprisingly, what the content of such preaching ought to be frequently occupies much of our time. Sometimes I hear assertions:

> What we need is the good old-fashioned Gospel!
> We ought to preach what is in the Bible!
> We want the Gospel, not Theology!
> Preaching must be relevant to people!

Sometimes I hear questions:

> Is the Gospel the same for every age?
> What is the Gospel for today?
> How does the Gospel relate to other religions?
> How can we communicate the Gospel in a secular age?

After having tried in my modest way to accept or reject the assertions and to answer the questions it

9

occurred to me that it might be of benefit to preachers generally if the job could be properly done by experts, and in print. This book is the result. It is too small for its subjects, but probably the right size for most of its readers. The authors would, of course, resist the suggestion that they are experts. Even so, we profit from the thinking they have done.

As in past issues of *The Preacher's Handbook*, the authors submit to no test for orthodoxy. They are free to say what they wish in their own way. The corollary of this freedom is that the Local Preachers' Department must not be taken as necessarily subscribing to opinions which are too radical for conservatives or too conservative for radicals.

About Preaching, Number One in the New Series, enjoyed a favourable reception. It would be an undeserved misfortune for the authors if *About the Gospel* did not do the same.

The Gospel and Theology

W. David Stacey

LET US BEGIN by disposing of two ever-popular errors that cannot even be accorded the honour of half-truths. The first is that the Gospel and theology have nothing to do with each other. The Gospel is the pure, living Word of God, preached by the converted to the convertible and issuing in justification, sanctification and assurance. Theology is the subtle and deceptive word of man. It is purveyed by the knowledgeable to embarrass the simple. It complicates and obscures what is essentially straightforward. It emasculates preaching by robbing it of its glorious directness. It insists, instead, on technicalities, cautious language, and endless qualifications. It is only necessary to say in reply that 'living', 'Word of God', 'converted', 'justification', 'sanctification' and 'assurance' are all theological terms of immense complexity. Without theology, nothing positive can be said about God or man or Christ and, of course, preaching could not take place at all. It is always annoying when someone else's mental patterns are more complicated than one's own, but this situation has to be faced. If an enquirer in the restaurant at the Central Hall asks two friends the way to Kingsway, one of them may sketch Whitehall and the Strand in pencil on a napkin and reckon that he has answered the question. The other may draw a detailed map—or produce somebody else's—showing all the side turnings and the one way streets. It is up to the enquirer which he chooses, but the first man cannot say, 'Well, I don't believe in maps', since he has just drawn one.

The second error, perhaps a little more sophisticated than the first, is that the Gospel actually is theology, that is to say, it is one, particular theological statement that is absolutely true, all other theological statements being, by obvious implication, false. There was a time, a decade or so ago, when theological students used to sit in judgement on the great preachers of the day. Their offerings would be labelled either 'the truth' or, more commonly, 'heresy'. The students were not as concerned as, perhaps, they might have been at the fact that, on this reckoning, there seemed to be precious little 'truth' around. This notion that the Gospel is a single, completely accurate, and final, theological statement no doubt has its attractions, but it must be resisted for a number of reasons.

First of all, it is quite impossible to sustain inside Methodism. We have no doctrinal standards of the kind that would give rise to such definitive theology. The doctrinal clauses in the Deed of Union are anything but precise: the statements of Faith and Order accepted by the Conference are models of comprehensiveness: and other official publications, like the Methodist Hymn-Book and the Book of Offices, express theological views of bewildering variety. The hard-liner who believes in 'truth' and 'heresy' just has no home in Methodism. That, of course, is not something to be sorry about. Exclusiveness in theology has cloaked more spiritual pride and done more harm to Christendom than any of us will ever know. We have great cause to be grateful that our founder did not hang this mill-stone round our necks.

Secondly, the devotees of the full, perfect and true theology are guilty of intellectualizing the Gospel. It has always been our boast that a man could enter the Kingdom of Heaven with whatever brains he'd got. A life committed to Jesus is a life committed to Jesus. It is faith in its own right. It does not have to express itself in certain propositions to be valid. Consequently, there have been many devoted Christian people whose theological ideas, when put under a microscope, proved to be a tangle of vague sentiments and inconsistencies, not to mention superstitions. Doubtless this is regrettable, but God did not make the whole human race capable of rigorous intellectual discipline. If we wanted uniformity of theology in Methodism, it could only be done by insisting that authentic pronouncements should be learnt by heart, which is absurd since we have no such pronouncements nor the will to learn them. There is no need to argue more. The case is a very unfashionable one these days. We must press on to find a middle road and examine it in some detail.

What, then, is the Gospel and what is theology? Fundamentally, the Gospel is not doctrines, state-

ments or words of any kind. It is an energy, a *dynamis*,
that issues from Christ and flows into the lives of
ordinary men. The woman with the haemorrhage in
Mark 5 is typical of those who encounter Jesus. She
first hears about him in v. 27 and there is no need to
suppose that what she heard was necessarily true or
perceptive. She heard enough to stimulate her interest.
She then went and encountered the man, touched his
garment, and the power of Jesus transformed her.
Now it must be readily granted that there is a basic
difference between this encounter situation in *Mark*
and the modern preaching situation, that in one Jesus
is represented as present physically, in the other he is
present in some other way, but it remains true that the
essential factor in both situations is the transmission
of power. Believing on the Lord Jesus Christ does not
mean passing an examination in Nicene Christology; it
means receiving from Christ his love, his forgiveness,
his stimulus, and accepting these things as of final and
ultimate value. No account of the preaching situation
is adequate that does not give priority to this factor,
which is one reason, as we have seen, why intellectualizing the Gospel is a disaster.

None the less, the Gospel must have a verbal form.
The very comparison we have made between *Mark* 5
and the modern pulpit situation underlines this. Physical presence must be replaced by some other kind of
presence, and, however strongly we may believe in
sacramental presence, the necessity of words is in-
escapable. Christ must make his appearance now
through words spoken about him. So the Gospel is
reduced to words. But there is still an important dis-

tinction between Gospel and theology. The Gospel is the passionate communication of the reality of Christ in the person to person context, the faith, sincerity, integrity of the preacher being as important as the words he uses. Theology is the cool, balanced, careful out-working of that reality in objective terms. The distinction must not be pushed too far. The preacher must think and the theologian must be sincere, but it is fair to say that personal qualities predominate in preaching the Gospel and technical skill is a *sine qua non* in writing theology.

One other point must be made while we are still talking about the distinction between Gospel and theology. It concerns the range of the two words. The Gospel is about the encounter with Christ. Millions of people have heard it and responded to it without considering much beyond that encounter. Theology cannot be so simple. Sooner or later, enquiring minds are going to tease out of this situation all kinds of very complicated questions. What does the encounter with Christ imply regarding Baptism, or Hell, or the Virgin Birth? Theology must answer such questions credibly, lucidly and consistently. Theology, therefore, must have an enormous range that the Gospel, in its simplicity, does not have.

So much for the distinction between the two. We must now look into the matter more deeply and we shall find that, useful as the distinction is, it is impossible to carry it right through. Passion and sincerity in preaching are fine, but you have got to use some words and nobody could possibly imagine that the choice of words was a matter of no consequence. But, and this is the real point, differing words can be used for differing situations. Different theologies can be constructed by different people for different functions. There is no, one, set pattern. Preaching to Jews, it was very reasonable to say that Jesus was Messiah, because the Jews understood about the Messiah and they knew what kind of thing was being asserted in the statement, 'Jesus is Messiah'. Those Gentiles who were completely outside the influence of Judaism would find the statement meaningless. To them the preacher must say, 'Jesus is Lord'. 'Messiah' and 'Lord' are two quite different words with very different meanings, so, formally speaking, the preacher is not making the same statement to Gentiles as he made to Jews. No, he has found the need to re-cast his theology, though, dynamically speaking, the Gospel he is proclaiming is the same in both cases. The conclusion is that, though the Gospel, in its personal and dynamic sense, stays the same, the theological terms in which it is expressed will vary from circumstance to circumstance.

What changes in circumstance lead to variations in theology? The best way to answer that question is to give examples. In the first place, one must consider the spirit of the age, what one might call the mood of the times. Compare the first decade of this century with the one that began in 1940. The Victorian age had produced the appearance of a great advance. Thousands of square miles had been added to the British Empire. British influence was extended more widely than ever before. Africa was being 'opened up', largely by Europeans. Industrial invention was heralding a new day. There was a widespread, though not universal, optimism about the affairs of men. 'The evangelization of the world in this generation' was the slogan. The decade reached its climax for Christians in the Edinburgh Missionary conference of 1910, one of the most hopeful assemblies that Christendom had ever seen. 1940 could tell a different story. The wickedness and incompetence of man had been exposed in two world wars. His inventive genius was now turned towards greater and greater destruction. Europe was enduring the worst tyranny she had ever known. The far flung countries had not yet succeeded in rejecting the white man, but the pattern of the future could be clearly foreseen. As far as the Church was concerned, membership had been falling steadily all through the century and influence had been declining even faster. Is it surprising therefore, that the theology of the first decade was liberal, buoyant and optimistic, that it built on the good in man and held high hopes of progress, whereas the theology of the war years in this country tended to despair of natural man, looked for hope to another dimension and turned back to the Bible doctrines of sin and redemption? To ask which of these theologies is true is to ask the wrong question. Each spoke to its time. Through each the power of Christ went out into the world, though, at many points, they are in formal contradiction.

Again one has to consider the audience. The substitution of 'Lord' for 'Messiah' was but one detail of the adaptation of the Gospel to the Gentile world. The whole statement had to be changed, not simply translated, but re-stated in a new idiom. This is a problem that missionaries still have to face. It took some time for the Church to grasp that the African could be a Christian as an African, and for a few decades the work of converting had to be accompanied by a process of Europeanization. To understand the Gospel one had to understand the way that the European Christian looked at life. This was an extraordinary bit of arrogance on the part of Europe. It seemed to be assumed that Christianity was native to our nineteenth-century civilization, for apparently it never occurred to those missionaries that they ought to try to understand how the first century Jew looked at life. Nowadays things are different. African Christianity, if we may generalize, is an expression of the Faith in its own right. And with African Christianity goes African theology. It does not have to be comprehensible to us and it does not have to be true in any timeless and spaceless sense. It can still be the right theology to express the Gospel in that time and that place.

Again one has to consider that the theologian himself changes. Not only is he alive in a changing world—many who are now preaching have actually lived through the changes I have described above—but he is a growing person. Growth, of course, is a great mystery and it could be discussed for ever, but I take it to involve at least two elements that are beyond denial. First it means a change in one's attitude to life. The splendour of youth is its vigour, its optimism, its enthusiasm. There are no problems that cannot be solved. Life has a certain simplicity. We, the rest of us, just have to stir ourselves up and get on with living it. Middle age brings more caution, more sense of tragedy and more patience. Will the same theological pattern suffice? One hopes not. Now it may be said that these statements about youth and age are broad generalizations that are not true in my case or your case or anyone's case. This may be so, but, in fact, it does not weaken the argument. We are simply contending that there is a difference between youth and age, not that we have correctly characterized it. As long as any difference in outlook is recognized, it is bound to be reflected in a difference in theology. A second factor is that growth means gathered knowledge. The more books one reads, the more talks one hears, the more conversations one has, the more the memory is stocked with ideas. Reasons for and against this or that slowly assemble themselves over the years, and one finds at last that one can no longer go on saying what one has always said about Hell or about the Kingdom of God or about other religions, simply because the weight of argument has altered. This is growth, this is wisdom, this is subtlety. It is to be applauded and not, as commonly, deplored. We have so far misunderstood the function of theology as to suggest that any significant change in a man's theological expression is a sign of weakness, spiritual failure, or even downright treachery. Almost the reverse is true. If there is no theological evolution, it suggests that there is no growth, or, worse, that there is growth, but it has no bearing on the expression of the Christian Faith. Unfortunately, this is sometimes true. People go on saying childish prayers all their lives. They go on purveying a naive theology throughout their pulpit ministry. There may be other reasons for this that are outside our brief. Here, however, we must make it clear that resistance to change in theological expression is not virtuous but is more probably based on a misapprehension of what theology is.

Perhaps even more difficult for some will be the contention that theological expression has to change according to the mental capacity of the people involved. A statement that is theologically 'true' in a Youth Club may be theologically 'untrue' in a senior common room. It is easy to say that all men have the same need of the Gospel, but not at all easy to see how this works out in practice. In theory the only thing that stops any man accepting the Gospel is sin, but the very idea of sin can be discussed on many different levels. There is a statement of the Christian understanding of sin that makes sense to the philosopher or the psychologist, but it is a different statement from that which accompanies most evangelical appeals. Again, this is not something to be deplored. Men are not all the same. Their mental patterns are not equally complex. Some minds are more analytical, more perceptive, than others. They will not be satisfied by the same theology. This is, perhaps, more readily grasped if we consider one particular area as an example, say the doctrine of Heaven. Now we all know what the simple message of heaven is and it has sustained and still sustains millions of Christians. In that very important sense the simple message is true. But there may be people who are bothered by the application of a linear time sequence to a nonspatial world, who find the very idea of personal exist-

ence in a non-physical medium to be problematic.
The answer to such people is not to tell them to
repent, but to think hard to meet their difficulties
with a theological statement that is not open to these
objections. This statement will also be true, though it
may be in formal contradiction of the other one.
Many different theologies—different, that is, in their
level of complexity—may be positive to different sec-
tors of the community. The simple preacher and the
learned theologian are both positive in their respective spheres and it is a great mistake to suggest that
the theology of one ought to conform to that of the
other.

The conclusion from this is that every man must
work out his own theology, that he must be prepared
to vary it as circumstances and, particularly, his
audience alters, and that he must be prepared to
revise his theology again and again as he himself
grows more mature. This is asking rather a lot from
the ordinary Christian member, though it is unwise to
under-rate his theological interest. But it is not asking
too much of the preacher. For him it is necessity. For
him fossilized theology is the great danger. Now it
may be said, against all this, that we need an unchanging theology to express the eternal Christian
verities, and it might be added, rather hesitantly, that
the Roman Catholics seem to have one and seem to
profit from it. To this there are two answers—apart
from what has been said already. First, we, in
Methodism, do not use theology in the way that it is
used in the Roman Church and, therefore, our
theology is not of the same kind as theirs. We have

very little dogmatic theology in Methodism, that is to say, theology promulgated by the Church and required to be believed by all its members. What we do have is a number of working theologies used in an almost functional way by our preachers. This pattern has served us well. It has not always been easy to say what the Methodist view of this or that was, but the pattern has sustained our community life very well. It is hard to believe that the people who press for an unchanging theology really want dogmatic theology on the Roman model. Do they really wish to be bound by the Conference in what they believe? It seems more likely that what they really want is the official adoption of their own theology. A large number of people seem to want that, which makes the whole thing absurd. Secondly, we need to ask ourselves very bluntly whether it is the eternal Christian verities that need the fixed theology or whether it is not rather our own mental inflexibility. The Faith has managed down through the centuries with a number of different theologies and has survived undiluted. It seems capable of being born and re-born in an infinite number of places and periods and cultures and languages and life-styles. Maybe you and I are not quite so flexible. We would like things tied down. That would be personally very attractive, but universally disastrous.

So we return to the necessity for the preacher constantly to re-think his theology, and the rest of this article must be devoted to that process. We will go through the method point by point, giving illustrations and noting the problems and the controversial areas as they arise.

The first question is where to begin. Do you begin with a concrete situation or with a load of ideas? It depends upon what purpose theology is to serve. The Church needs practical theologians who spend all their time bringing the Gospel to bear on matters like medical ethics and industrial relations, and, even more, bringing the Gospel to individual people in individual situations. It also needs theoreticians who relate all the practical theologies of the moment to the great Christian traditions and work out a massive, consistent theological system that comprehends them all. Which function can you and I fulfil? The question will not take most of us long to answer. Theology of the second kind is quite vital to the life of a Church, but it calls for very special gifts. Fortunately a relatively small number of systematic theologians can maintain the theological vitality of a large Christian body. At no time has Methodism boasted more than a handful of theoreticians of this kind, and few of us will imagine ourselves included in their number. We are the practical theologians, and that, surely, gives us the point at which we begin.

We begin with an actual situation. Who am I and who are the people I am addressing myself to? I may be a young school-teacher addressing a young people's group. I may be an elderly farmer preaching to a dozen faithful and experienced souls. I may be a factory worker arguing with my peers in the canteen. I may even be a parent discussing things with my children. Each is a situation to which the Gospel is relevant and where theological ideas must be expressed, but, clearly, they are all different. Each is a critical situation, because, in every case, the participants think the confrontation important. There are matters to be discussed, but, more than that, they are all situations in which the 'energy' of the Gospel can be released. Now it ought to be clear without further argument that the importation into any of these situations of a Christian system of ideas simply because it is a Christian—and therefore, presumably, correct—system is a mistake. The hope, the possibility of the situation lies in the encounter, the meeting of people with things in common. To take the third example, Joe, the unbeliever, is interested in arguing with Bill, the Christian, because they are both being called out on strike and the rights and wrongs of industrial action are such a complicated business that the whole issue has to be looked at again and again from every point of view. Bill, as a Christian, may have something to offer. What is quite certain is that he cannot offer what most people call Christian theology. The whole thing is about human sin, no doubt, but, if all Bill can do is to say that all men are born in sin and have need of a Saviour, Jesus Christ, neither Joe nor anybody else will listen to him. Static theology cannot be wheeled in in this way. The same applies to all the examples, even the one of the farmer and his congregation. Granted that Christian worship is different from the other situations cited, it is still related directly to living. Theological and biblical orations by one whose expertise is in farming do not make Christian worship edifying. They merely push it fur-

ther and further into the realm of the irrelevant. If the
farmer and his congregation could only realize that
they share in a village community that experiences all
the joys and the crises that flesh is heir to and which
they know from the inside and which they have tried
to approach in faith, then they could share in
Christian worship that actually presents this world—
and not some other—to God. It takes a farmer to work
out the theology of agricultural life. The theory can
safely be left to the bachelors of divinity.

Every situation throws up points of crisis. The
practical theologian has to make straight for them. In
theory these all ought to be due to sin and all one
ought to need to say is, 'Repent'. In practice the
crises are more often crises of confusion rather than
guilt and the problem is whom to say, 'Repent' to
and about what. This needs further elaboration.
Many of us older preachers will remember the days
when evangelical appeals were often successful, when
people did weep for their sins, or so it seemed. We
may, therefore, suppose that sin is still sin and that
the reason that few people weep about it now is that
they are too brazen or that they do not have their sin
pointed out to them with the same force as in the old
days. But another explanation is possible. It may be
that the sense of guilt felt by anyone is the result
largely of social pressures. The preacher may think
that it is his stirring word that leads to the public
confession whereas in fact he merely provides the occasion on which the guilt that society has engendered
breaks out. Once the social pressures change, the
sense of guilt changes. Now this is surely what has

happened. Our fathers, brought up amid Victorian prudery, were loaded with guilt. They felt themselves constantly in need of repentance, particularly from sexual misdemeanours, and they were consequently attentive when preachers alluded to their secret sins. Things are quite different now. A generation is rising now that does not understand this pressure. Private, inner guilt is not the crisis. It may be that social guilt for the injustices of society and the world will, in a decade or two, replace private guilt, but that has not happened yet. At the moment, among the young, the crisis is confusion rather than guilt. This is the place where our theology has got to begin. We have got to provide clear, reliable, sane and just guide-lines to people who are in doubt. That is a theological task to keep us all busy.

It may be objected, in passing, that the last paragraph is wrongly argued. Sin, it may be said, *is* the problem. The Bible says so. Our fathers were right and our children are wrong. To this it can be replied briefly that no modern society can reproduce exactly the biblical sense of sin. The Victorians have no better claim than the hippies, in some ways, a worse one. The Gospel is the power of God in 1971 to those alive in 1971. It does not need to wear Victorian clothes. Nor does the Bible. It is hard to make the Bible speak to our age, but it always was. It was no easier one hundred years ago.

At this point we could have a useful discussion on language. Does theology require a particular vocabulary and must we expect those who may listen to us to learn it? Again, it depends upon what kind of theology we are talking about. The systematic theology we described four paragraphs back is a highly complex study and it certainly requires technical terms of its own. But the practical theology, the shop floor theology we have been describing since, is a different matter. One cannot expect too much co-operation. If we become difficult to listen to, we shall find ourselves talking to ourselves. The great communicators have always begun at the point of crisis and used language that could be understood. That is the method. But their point of crisis and their language will not do for us. We have to find our own. Far too much preaching fails because it is in what amounts to a foreign tongue. It is crowded with terms that common speech left behind years ago. We still have plenty of preachers who have real empathy with their workmates, who can speak the language of the factory and the terraces; and it is inexpressibly sad to find that, when they mount the pulpit steps, they start talking like dusty ecclesiastics. After making allowances for the flippancy and vulgarity that one would not want in worship, the language of the man is the language of his theology. To put it from the other side, people who have no idea what the word 'Messiah' means in the street will not understand it when it is spoken from the pulpit.

We move on to consider the aim of practical theology. It is, by our original definition, to express the power of the Gospel in a precise situation. How will that power show itself? The answer to this question is very significant. It reveals one of the tensions within the word 'theology'. Are we attempting to convince people in the Gospel that certain ideas are true, or are we trying to bring them to a new kind of living? Now of course we are trying to do both, because they are inseparable, but which has priority? In terms of practical theology, it is the new life that we are after. Get them loving their neighbour first and talk about realized eschatology afterwards. Every practical theologian knows this to be true. If the crisis point is, say, a question of whether to have an abortion, the practical problem has to be solved first. Elucidation of Christian ideas of the value of human life and then the application of those ideas to the precise situation will answer no questions at all. The entire matter will be seen by those involved simply in terms of one particular embryo. The middle aged couple who say, 'All right, let's have him and love him', are making a profoundly theological remark, though it would not be found in the text-books. And it is the practical situation, not arm-chair reasoning that gives rise to it.

All practical theology leads towards systematic theology. Man is, to some extent, a reasoning animal and he will not be content to leave behind him a string of crises without trying to make some rational pattern, out of the various decisions to which he came. It is a hard struggle, because new decisions sometimes appear and spoil the emerging pattern, but it is a necessary one. So the Gospel, which expresses itself first in courageous actions, comes to a theological form. Theology is first done and then thought about. Then new circumstances call for it to be done again, and thought about again. And so it goes on and will go on as long as men continue to live by faith.

The Gospel in the New Testament

Robert Way-Rider

THE ORIGINAL preachers of the Gospel were Peter and his companions, Jews who lived in first century Palestine. Before they began to preach they had spent some time with Jesus and they preached in the first place to other Jews in Palestine. These facts provide the reasons for a number of aspects of the message which Peter and the others preached and which many passages in the New Testament illustrate. These facts show why when they began to preach the Christian message they based their preaching on the Old Testament. This was both natural and necessary under the circumstances, since both preachers and hearers were Jews and so steeped in the Old Testament Scriptures. Jesus himself, who had prepared these men for their task, knew the Old Testament intimately and used it often.

These first Christian preachers, addressing hearers in Palestine, took the understanding of the Old Testament which they shared with their fellow Jews as the basis for their preaching, but gave it a new slant and emphasis. We must begin with this understanding of the Old Testament in order to appreciate the special emphasis which the Christian preachers of the New Testament gave to it. Basically they saw the Old Testament as describing a series of God's mighty acts in history. These mighty acts were part of God's plan, which was not yet complete.

This view of history developed during the period of time covered in the Old Testament. Its beginning seems to have been in the events of the Exodus from Egypt of the descendants of Abraham. These people came to believe that God had promised them a land in which they could settle, and their original understanding of God's purpose seemed to go no further than this. A passage which illustrates this original view of Israel's history is Dt 26:5-9. This passage contains an account of the Exodus event for the Israelite to repeat in the sanctuary at the celebration of the Harvest Festival in the period soon after the Israelites entered Canaan, and there are many similar passages. In these passages we find a pattern of events:

The Election of the Fathers (Abraham, etc.)
The Affliction in Egypt
God's Deliverance or Call
The Covenant or Promise
The Fulfilment of the Promise, i.e. the Gift of the Land.

Other passages which illustrate this pattern are Ex 15:1-18; Dt 7:1-11; 29:1ff (which lacks the fulfilment).

Most of the events in this list are represented in Dt 26:5-9, although it does not mention the Covenant between God and his people at Sinai. This pattern of events formed the original nucleus which developed further during Israel's history.

The next stage in the development of this pattern came in the time of the eighth and seventh century prophets before the Exile. Their teaching took the pattern of events beyond the gift of the Land and commented on what followed the settlement in Canaan. These prophets added two, sometimes three items to the list. They described the events after the Settlement as unfaithfulness and rebellion on Israel's part, which must be followed by God's judgement on his unfaithful people. Some prophets went further than this, however:

Israel's Rebellion and Unfaithfulness
God's Judgements on His People
Gods' Promise of Restoration (especially in Hosea and in Jeremiah's idea of the New Covenant).

Passages which illustrate the development under the prophets include Joel 2:28-3:2; Am 2:6-16; 3:1 f; 9:7 f. Passages showing the idea of Restoration after the Judgements include Ho 11:8-12; Jer 31:31 ff; 32:32-52:33 passim. This was the understanding of her history which Israel took with her into exile.

After the Exile the development of the Confessional Pattern, as we may call it, continued. Because God's people came to see that God was the only God of all the earth they added the Creation at the beginning of the pattern of events which revealed his purpose. They also came to lay great stress on the promise of Restoration. It may be that the difficulties of resettling in Palestine after the Exile led them to feel that something better still lay ahead for them. There is a very fine example of this extended form of the Confessional Pattern in the prayer of Neh 9 : 6-38.

9 : 6	Creation
9 : 7f	Election of Abraham
9 : 9	Affliction in Egypt
9 : 10-12	Deliverance from Egypt
9 : 13f	Covenant at Sinai
9 : 16-23	Wanderings in the Wilderness
9 : 24f	Gift of the Land
9 : 26-31	Rebellion and Judgement
9 : 32-7	Present Condition of the People
9 : 38	Renewal of the Covenant.

This prayer, like the prayer in Dt 26:5 ff, is obviously modelled on the outline of Israel's history to be found in the Confession Pattern. But a comparison of the two passages shows how far the outline has been extended forwards and backwards since the settlement in the Promised Land. Jahweh who brought the people out of Egypt is now the Creator of heaven and earth, with a name too holy to be used in speech. Since the settlement in Canaan he has continued his mighty acts in bringing his judgements on Israel for their unfaithfulness, but he has promised to restore them when their punishment is at an end. This passage in Nehemiah represents the climax of the development of the summary of Israel's history which forms the framework of the Confessional Pattern in the Old Testament.

From the period of the Return from Exile the people never lost sight of this idea that God would act again in history to restore Israel. This is one reason for the development of the Messianic hope which lay behind the fierce anticipation of this Restoration in the period of Roman domination during which Jesus lived and during which the life of the Church began.

We find the use of the Confessional Pattern in a number of New Testament passages. Examples are the sermons or speeches in Acts, such as Ac 2:14-40; 3:12-26; 7:2-53; 13:16-41; and elsewhere in Ro 15:9-12; 2 Co 6:16-8; Heb 1:1-4; 11:1-end; 1 Pet 2:1-10. The New Testament writers, like the first Christian preachers, claimed that Jesus was the fulfilment of Israel's hope of Restoration. Their original message, as we find it reflected in the sermons of the early chapters of Acts, runs somewhat like this:

The Scriptures are fulfilled
In Jesus the Messiah
    in his life and ministry
    in his sufferings and death
    in his resurrection and ascension
    in his return and judgement.
The Holy Spirit in the Church is the sign of Christ's
    present power and glory
The Apostles are witnesses of these things
Repent and be baptized and you will receive the
    forgiveness of your sins.

This message clearly follows quite naturally from

the promise of Restoration with which the later form of the Confessional Pattern ends. The very first Christian preachers, working in Palestine and using their own Jewish background, clearly felt that they were proclaiming the continuance of the purpose which God had begun to carry out long ago in the life of his people Israel.

To make it even more clear to their hearers how Jesus was the fulfilment of the Scriptures they used four groups of passages from the Old Testament from which they frequently quoted. The passages in each group share a theme which relates to the Christian message outlined above. The groups are these:

I. Scriptures of the Day of the Lord and the Coming of the Lord.

These include Joel 2 and 3; Zech 9-14; Dan 7.

II. Scriptures of the New Israel.

These include Hosea; Is 6:1-9:7; 11:1-10; 28:16; 40:1-11; Jer 31:10-34.

III. Scriptures of the Servant of the Lord and the Righteous Sufferer.

These include Is 42:1-44:5; 49:1-13; 50:4-11; 52:13-53:12; 61:1-end; Ps 22; 31; 34; 38; 41; 42-3; 69; 80; 88; 118.

IV. Scriptures of the Messiah.

These include Ps 2; 110; Is 55:3.

During the period before Paul began his work in Asia Minor on his first missionary journey the Church used these four groups of Old Testament Passages, which we may call *Testimony Passages*, to support the claims made in its message, which is called the

Kerygma or Preaching. This *Kerygma* describes the fulfilment of the expectation in the *Confessional Pattern* that God would restore Israel. The *Kerygma* emphasises the events of the earthly life of Jesus and presents Jesus as a man. During this period before the Gentile mission Christians called Jesus Son of David, Servant, Messiah.

All this was obviously most useful in commending Jesus in Palestine and Syria. This approach helped Christian preachers to present Jesus in terms which their hearers could understand and accept. Ac 13:16-41 shows that this approach was also useful when Paul preached in the synagogues of Asia Minor. The further west Paul went in his missionary work, however, the fewer synagogues there were and the more he had to preach directly to Gentiles who had no knowledge of Judaism at all. Paul had to face a very real problem at this stage in his work. He had to find a way of making this *Kerygma* and its associated passages from the Old Testament meaningful to people who knew nothing about the Old Testament, and who had a quite different background of ideas from those of Judaism. Paul's greatness as a missionary preacher appeared in the way he solved this problem. He modified the framework of the *Kerygma* a little and the vocabulary a great deal, and he omitted the Old Testament references.

The form of the *Kerygma* addressed to Gentiles we can set down somewhat like this:

The purpose of God is fulfilled
In Jesus the Lord
    Who became man

Who died for you and for all
Whom God has raised and exalted
Who will come to be our Judge
The Apostles are his witnesses.

Believe in him and be baptized and you will receive the Holy Spirit.

Paul has modified the framework very little. He has had to make the reference to the Holy Spirit part of the closing appeal, and that for a very good reason. Christians in Palestine could point to the Spirit-filled communities of disciples which existed after Pentecost; Christian preachers in Asia Minor and in Greece could not. During this period, however, there is evidence that Gentile converts received the Holy Spirit at their baptism, e.g. Ac 10:44-8; 19:1-7. This makes it quite natural to refer the work of the Holy Spirit to the final part of the *Kerygma* as the result of response to the appeal.

The accounts in Acts of Christian preaching where the hearers are predominantly Gentile show how the *Kerygma* takes here a different form. Even Peter's sermon to the household of Cornelius shows something of this change. It is of about the same length as his sermon in Ac 3:12-26 addressed to the crowd in the Temple, but has only one quite general reference to the prophets (Ac 10:42). The sermon in Ac 3:12 ff, on the other hand, has three definite citations of Old Testament passages and a number of Old Testament allusions. Also while Ac 3:19 calls on the Jewish crowd in the Temple to repent Ac 10:43 speaks in terms of 'everyone who believes'. When we remember that according to Ac 10:2 Cornelius and his household were synagogue adherents who should be expected to know at least something of the Old Testament this is all the more noticeable as evidence of the way Christian preachers accommodated their message to Gentile hearers. Another example of this accommodation is in the words of Paul and Barnabas to the people of Lystra in Ac 14:15 ff. Luke has given here only the beginning of the sermon, but even this is clearly different from the sermons to Jewish hearers in Ac 2-5.

An example of Paul's letters of this approach to Gentiles is Col 1:24-8. There are references here to a number of elements of the *Kerygma* but these elements appear in a very different dress from the one they wear in Ac 2 or Ro 1:1-6. A briefer example from another writer concerned to commend the Gospel to the Gentiles is 1 Jn 4:9 f. In all the passages mentioned in this paragraph Christian writers are saying the same thing. They say it in one way to Jews and in another way to Gentiles.

Because they used these two approaches it is clear that Paul and other New Testament writers had to make use of a completely different vocabulary for the Gentile form of the *Kerygma*. Some examples of this new approach in Paul's letters are Phil 2:7-10; 3:8-11; Col 1:12-19, 25, 28 f; 2:9-13. Paul replaced 'Christ' or 'Messiah' with the universally familiar 'Lord', a word used of pagan deities and of the Roman emperor. He replaced the appeal to the Scriptures by speaking of the purpose of God, a concept already familiar in the Gentile world. By using this more familiar vocabulary Paul made the *Kerygma* a message which the Gentiles could more easily understand and so accept. It is because of this change of language that the Christian mission of the first century led to the establishing of Christianity as a world religion. It was because Christians of this time were ready to speak the language of their hearers that they could commend Jesus to the Gentile world with such success.

The Gentiles who became Christians arrived at a different understanding of Jesus from the understanding reflected in the Jewish form of the *Kerygma*. There the emphasis was on the humanity of Jesus. In the Gentile Church there came to be more emphasis on the divine aspect of his nature. Converts who previously used 'Lord' of pagan deities now used it of Jesus and thought that he must be at least as good as the gods they previously worshipped. The name 'Son of man' which Jesus used of himself was replaced in the Gentile Church by 'Son of God'. Because Gentile Christians lay more emphasis on the divine aspect of the nature of Jesus they came to think of him as pre-existing before his Incarnation. This is the reason why the Synoptic Gospels with their Palestinian background begin with the infancy or with the public ministry of Jesus while the much later Fourth Gospel refers to the pre-existing Word who became flesh (Jn 1 : 14). During the period between the origin of the Gospel tradition and the writing of the Fourth Gospel the Gentile Church had grown up and reached an understanding of Jesus which stressed his divinity.

The Gentile Christians came to think of Jesus as first pre-existent, then becoming incarnate as a man and after his death being exalted once more to be with God and thus to resume his divinity. This development of belief about Jesus had its influence on the use of the Old Testament within the Church, since although the Scriptures were not used in evangelism they played a part in worship and in the instruction given to converts. Christians who came to think of Jesus as pre-existent found in the Old Testament a number of passages where they saw reference to the activity of the pre-existent Jesus in events which the Old Testament described, such as the call of Abraham and of Moses, the Deliverance from Egypt and even the Creation. 1 Co 10:1-5 is an example of this new application of the Old Testament. By interpreting Old Testament passages in this way Christians came to think of Jesus as himself preparing beforehand for his earthly ministry. Because these passages are concerned with this attempt to find the real presence of Jesus in Old Testament events they are called *Real Presence Passages*. Examples of these passages are Gen 12, 15, 17, 18; Ex 2, 3; Dt 9, 10; Ps 8, 24; Hab 2:1-4. Two Real Presence Passages used to support the view that Jesus had a ministry to the Gentiles are Ps 19 and Is 49:1-9.

Thus by the end of the New Testament period the Church had a Gospel in two forms, a Jewish *Kerygma* and a Gentile *Kerygma* which had developed from it and influenced the Jewish material. Both forms were of service to the Church at this time. The Jewish form was useful both in preaching to the Jews and in defending the Christian faith against Jewish attacks by using the Old Testament. It formed a permanent part of the resources of the Church.

The Gentile form of the *Kerygma* was vital for the outreach of the Church to the world along the north and south coasts of the Mediterranean, where Christians penetrated to areas where Judaism was almost or quite unknown. Here Christian preachers won converts by putting over with a different vocabulary what was basically the same message as that originally preached to Jews in Palestine. It was this form which in turn provided the basis for the historic creeds which developed in the later centuries of the life of the Church.

Comparison of the Apostles' Creed with the *Kerygma* as set out above shows that it was the Gentile *Kerygma* which provided the underlying framework. There were additions to this original framework but these did not obscure the framework itself. The use of the Gentile form of the *Kerygma* here shows that it had long been accepted as an authoritative statement of Christian belief. This acceptance shows how successful this method of communicating the Christian faith was among people without a Jewish background. The success of this Gentile *Kerygma* is relevant to the preacher's task today.

One aspect which is most important to us is the way in which the first Christian preachers were ready to speak the language of their hearers rather than the language of their teachers. We can learn much from this in our situation. In conversation and in preaching we can put over our message much more helpfully by avoiding technical terms which we have inherited from the theology of a previous age, using in their place language from today's vocabulary. For example it is often more meaningful today to speak of failure or frustration than to speak of guilt. In the same way we can reach our hearers better when we speak of being reconciled than when we speak of being redeemed. Preachers today will find some valuable lessons for themselves when they consider how the New Testament preachers used a new vocabulary in order to reach new hearers.

We should also notice that this change extends in the New Testament far more to the vocabulary of Christian preaching than to its framework. The New Testament preachers altered the framework of the *Kerygma* only where it was necessary to do so in order to relate their message to the experience of converts from outside Judaism. Despite the new vocabulary the Gentile form of the *Kerygma* proclaimed essentially the same message as the earlier Jewish version. This too is a feature of the New Testament preachng from which we of today can learn. There is an essential core of Christian belief which the preacher must proclaim however much he adapts his language to the occasion and to his hearers. The two forms of the *Kerygma* in the New Testament show what are the themes which the first Christian preachers felt they could not abandon as they took the Gospel to the non-Jewish world. If we think of our own position as preachers today we can see how the same themes must form the basis of our own message. A further parallel between the situation of the New Testament period and that of

our own day is the way in which we have to put across
our message to a world which has little contact with
the Bible and with Biblical thought. An example of
how we might express the *Kerygma* in terms of today's
language would be as follows:

You can understand God through Jesus
> Who lived out God's love
> Who died to reconcile men to God
> Who is now with God
> Who will decide whether we survive death.

The Church continues what Jesus began to do
Trust yourself to him and you will receive his
power.

In the task of adapting the vocabulary of our message while retaining its essentials the New Testament
writers can teach us much.

Nor is this all the New Testament writers can teach
us about the best way to proclaim our message today.
We can learn from them how to emphasize the parts
of our message which have most appeal to our hearers,
just as the New Testament preachers did. The sermons
in the early part of Acts emphasize the Resurrection
of Jesus. This emphasis has considerable appeal to the
Eastern mind and continues in the thought and
worship of the Orthodox Church. When Paul came to
Greece, however, he found that the part of his message
which had the greatest impact on his hearers was the
Crucifixion of Jesus. He therefore emphasized this
rather than the Resurrection (c.f. 1 Co 1:17 and
1:23). We are preaching in a period when the earthly
life of Jesus seems to stimulate the interest of people

outside the Church. It may therefore well be necessary for us to stress his identification with us in his Incarnation. This is not to say that we shall abandon parts of the *Kerygma* which seem less relevant to our contemporaries. However, there is obviously wisdom in dealing most fully with those parts of the Christian message which arouse the greatest interest among people today.

Another way of adapting the *Kerygma* to the present situation is that suggested by Professor Rudolf Bultmann. Under the name of 'demythologizing' this has attracted a good deal of attention on both sides of the Atlantic. In trying to put Bultmann's approach in the simplest possible terms we may say that what he attempts to do is to express the Christian message in terms of a form of existentialist philosophy. Existentialism is a philosophical approach which tries to express philosophical truths in terms of human experience or existence. This is the reason why this philosophical approach is called 'existentialism'. A good deal has been written for and against this approach of Bultmann to the question of how best to communicate the Gospel in terms which modern man will find meaningful. From the preacher's point of view there are one or two points which it will be well to bear in mind. The first is that demythologizing as Bultmann undertakes it involves speaking the language of philosophy rather than the language of the man in the street. About this we may say that there is no more reason to expect the man in the street to understand philosophical terms than there is to expect him to understand Biblical phraseology. We may therefore be less than fully convinced that Bultmann has found the solution to the modern problem of communication. It is also possible to comment on the appropriateness of expressing the Christian message in terms of existentialist philosophy. Here it can be said that any philosophy which takes seriously the spiritual dimensions of human experience will serve as a means of expressing the Christian Gospel, but that its use is subsidiary to the main purpose of preaching. This is because the Gospel is in its essence not an attempt to formulate a philosophy but rather an attempt to say what God has done for us by means of Jesus. This is the aim of the New Testament preachers in the *Kerygma* and it is still the aim of the preacher today. However we attempt to express the central themes of the Christian Gospel it must be true for us as for the New Testament preachers that God was in Christ reconciling the world to himself and that he has committed to us the word of reconciliation.

The understanding of the New Testament *Kerygma* will help us to proclaim that word of reconciliation. In the first place it will help us to declare that history makes sense, that history has a pattern in it and a purpose behind it. This is what Biblical writers mean when they speak in terms of the mighty acts of God. Like the New Testament preachers we can declare that Jesus fulfils this purpose not only in his earthly life but also in the exalted life which follows his Resurrection. We can believe that this view of history finds support in the mind and teaching of Jesus himself. We can find indications of this in the accounts of his teaching in the Gospels, and particularly in the Passion

Predictions in Mark. Here we can go behind the Apostles to their Master.

In proclaiming this message we can follow the example of the New Testament writers in the way we express it. We can feel free to express our beliefs in language which our contemporaries can understand. In doing this we must take care to use contemporary language in order to express the essential core of Christian truth which the *Kerygma* represents. We may stress those elements in it which seem best to stimulate the interest of our contemporaries and to meet their need. At the same time we must remain faithful to this basic pattern.

The Shape of the Gospel in History

Robin E. Hutt

IN THE EDITORIAL of last year's Handbook, the editor, speaking of the first Christians, said: 'They believed that Christ meant them to stand up and proclaim what God had done and was doing for his people. So they did. And this obligation to preach—in whatever form—has been the ongoing responsibility of the Body of Christ ever since.'

The proclamation, therefore, has had two strands. The first is what God has done in the life of his people, as evidenced in the Bible, and in particular, what he has done in Jesus Christ. It is this that has given continuity throughout the centuries, despite many different forms of preaching. The second strand concerns the nature of the Gospel for each generation. How the fact of God in Christ is to be seen as good news depends upon the needs and conditions of the time. The history of preaching contains the story of how the Church has tried, with varying degrees of success, to proclaim 'what God has done and was doing', in a way that was seen to be relevant to each succeeding age. So we shall look at that story in barest outline, and see if it has anything to say to us about preaching today.

Before we go on however, one or two things must be borne in mind. First of all, it is impossible to assess what was preached in all the individual Christian churches throughout the years. We can only look at certain famous individuals, and general tendencies. Secondly, with such a broad topic being attempted in a few pages, sweeping generalizations are inevitable, as are large gaps in historical sequence. The books listed at the end will indicate the source of greater detail. Thirdly, attention has been focused almost entirely on the English Church.

From the Apostles to the Middle Ages

Some years ago Professor C. H. Dodd made a study of the preaching of the Apostles, and summarized their message under six headings[1]:

1. The promised Messianic Age has dawned.
2. It has come about through the life, death and resurrection of Jesus.
3. By virtue of the resurrection He has been exalted at the right hand of God.
4. The Holy Spirit in the Church is the sign of Christ's present power and glory.
5. Jesus will soon return and the Messianic Age will reach its consummation.
6. Therefore repent and believe.

This preaching was partly conditioned by the fact that

47

it was directed towards the unconverted, and also by
the firm belief that Jesus would return soon. As it
became clear that Our Lord's return was not as close
as expected, and as regular Christian congregations
became established, the proclamation developed into
what has been called 'Liturgical Preaching'. That is,
the sermon arose from the passages of scripture
read in the service, and took its place in the movement of the liturgy, culminating in the Communion.
In expounding the scriptures preachers were able to
proclaim what God had done, to instruct the congregation in the faith, and direct them towards a
moral and practical outworking of that faith in daily
living.

Two of the ablest exponents of this type of preaching were S. John Chrysostom of Constantinople, and
S. Ambrose of Milan. In *The Fathers of the Latin
Church* Dr Hans von Campenhausen gives some indication of the breadth and balance of Ambrose's
preaching in this summary of his views : '[the Church]
should above all proclaim "faith" and teach the
people to know God's holy will. God has redeemed us
in Christ and forgives us our sins. He demands that we
now likewise forgive, and as Christians conduct a life
of rigid discipline and sanctification. The church and
the Christian have also a social task. They must help
all the world's oppressed to obtain their rights, and
seek to relieve the distress of the poor to the best of
their ability. . . . The poor are the real treasure of the
church; it is unnecessary that she be also rich herself.'

The medieval period presents us with quite a different situation. Christianity had been established and

accepted for centuries. Life was coarse and hard for most people, with little education for the majority, including the ordinary parish clergy.

It is difficult to assess how frequently the common people of the Middle Ages heard sermons. Much would depend upon the local priest. He was not without help, and many books of homilies were produced to provide him with material. One of the most popular was even called *Dormi Secure* ('Sleep Soundly'—and don't worry about tomorrow's sermon!) There were of course the preaching Friars, trained preachers whose exuberant stories provided a lively contrast to the normally dull services in the parish church. There were also—by the fifteenth century—the 'Lollards', the followers of John Wyclif. The Friars had succumbed to their own popularity, and began to play to the gallery and to adopt a more luxurious way of life. This evoked the fierce criticism of Wyclif, and he and his school determined to preach a more biblically based and austere message. They translated the Bible into English and went out in pairs, in poverty, wearing a simple robe, and carrying a staff. Nevertheless, despite the preaching of the Friars and the Lollards, it remains true that outside the towns sermons were seldom heard.

How then did the Church fulfil its obligation to preach the Gospel? It did so partly through the words of the preacher, but also through the medium of Mystery Plays, through crude and colourful pictures, carvings and windows in churches, through the rich variety of activities associated with a full Church calendar of festivals and saints' days. Above all there was the Mass, with its high moment in the elevation of the bread for veneration as Christ's body.

Preaching was very often linked with these media. G. R. Owst gives us a picture of a preacher who '... seems to be actually reading off to us from the walls of some ancient Shropshire church, ... the fiend, pitch-black "as a man of Inde", with sharp nose, loathful face, and blazing eyes, blowing flames of fire from his mouth, the burning cauldron, the worms and adders that came out of it'.[2] This illustrates not only the crudeness of some of the pictures, but also the preoccupation of the period with the spectres of hell and the Devil. An over emphasis on the forgiving mercy of God encouraged the sinner in his sins, according to the medieval Church, so the preacher says: 'I trow there is no man that liveth, and he would consider inwardly what pain is ordained for sinners in hell, I trow it would dread him sore, and full soon amend him.'[3]

Processions were sometimes an occasion for preaching. They were a means of involving the whole community, and were associated with certain feast-days, or called in times of danger to pray for deliverance. One of the written homilies tells us that '... in these processions banners and crosses be borne, and bells rung, that the spirits that fly above in the air as thick as motes in the sun should flee away from us, when they see the banners and crosses aloft, and hearing the bells ring.'[4]

Indeed, much of the preaching of the period was concerned with matters of ritual and religious duties, and with general moral teaching. Typical themes were the meaning of the Mass, the reasons for and exhor-

tation towards the celebration of festivals and saints'
days, proper preparation for coming to Easter
Communion, the tasks of parents and servants, the
avoidance of witchcraft and superstition '. . . in short,
everything that the Church deemed needful for the
ordinary man and woman to know.'[5]

All this seems a far cry from the preaching of the
Apostles, but medieval England was a far cry from the
first century Roman Empire. No one questioned belief
in God, or the Lordship of Christ. The main elements
in the Christian Faith were regularly brought to mind
in the festivals of the Church calendar. What was
needed in addition was guidance in practical Christian
living, and the encouragement of regular prayer and
worship. 'In an age of wild manners, untamed pas-
sions, open vice, it is the glory of the Catholic Church
that she did clearly set herself to redeem the peasant
and labourer from the primitive errors of their ways
with direct, practical warnings and advice, wherever
such homely sermons were preached. They must be
judged in the light of what subsequent generations
have been able to accomplish towards gentler modes
of life and conduct, greater education and spiritual
achievement, among the masses. Without their quaint
thunder, their homely thrusts, their melodramatic nar-
rations to hold the rustics' attention to higher things,
our social progress might have been even slower.'[6]

It may be thought by some that the Gospel should
not be preached to further 'social progress', though
that might be one of its outworkings. But the truth is
that prevailing social conditions *must* influence the
way in which it is proclaimed, and the elements within

the Gospel which are particularly relevant to those conditions *must* be brought to the fore. That was true in the first century, it was true in the medieval period, it is also true in the more modern periods of history to which we now turn.

From Tillotson to Wesley

One of the most famous and popular English preachers was John Tillotson (1630-94) Archbishop of Canterbury. It was said of him by a friend: 'He was not only the best preacher of the age, but seemed to have brought preaching to perfection.'[7] He represents a new age, a new type of preaching.

Tillotson lived at a time when the Church was faced with a rapidly increasing range of scientific discovery, a questioning of miracle, mystery and dogmatism, and a collapse of public morals. What was necessary in his day was preaching which could demonstrate the relationship between faith and knowledge, reason and revelation, right doctrine and sound morals. G. R. Cragg says of this period: 'Within little more than a generation we pass from an atmosphere still predominately medieval to one which is essentially modern. The prevailing outlook changed. Questions emerged which still command our interest. We still discuss the place of reason, the nature of authority, the character of the universe, and we do so in the spirit which first appeared in the latter part of the 17th Century.'[8]

In such a time of transition, what was the aim and content of the preaching? It was avowedly to change men's nature by appeal to the reasonableness of Christianity. The Gospel came to Tillotson's contemporaries in terms of rationality and sensible precaution. It assured educated Christians disturbed by the new learning, of the good news that it was not unreasonable to believe in God, and that faith and obedience were not blind superstition. The most popular of Tillotson's sermons was on the text 'The Commandments of God are not Grievous' (1 John 5:3), which can be taken as a typical sermon of the period. The emphasis is that Christian obedience to duty and moral precepts makes for an easy life here, and assures one of a place in heaven. 'We have the greatest encouragement to the observance of God's commands. Two things make any course of life easy: present pleasure, and the assurance of future reward. Religion gives part of its reward in hand, the present comfort and satisfaction of having done our duty; and for the rest it offers us the best security that heaven can give. Now these two must needs make our duty very easy . . .' The standards God sets are all attainable, and only a little common sense is needed to see that it is so, and to combat our temptations: 'Our natural reason, if we will but listen to the dictate of it, is an enemy to all these sins, and a law against all these vices.'

Christ seems always to be the Example, and rarely the Saviour. The Gospel of the Kingdom became a sober, prudential, moral code of behaviour. The 'Gospel of Moral Rectitude' was apparently preached from every English pulpit at the beginning of the eighteenth century. The prevailing philosophy and conditions of the day, as ever, influenced the shape of the Gospel in Tillotson's time. The pervading laissez-faire attitude that everything in society is as it should be, that poverty is within the natural order (a notion which in some backwaters survives to this day), deprived the preaching of any prophetic note or far-reaching social concern, although in exhorting moral uprightness Tillotson could not avoid condemning the immorality and malpractices of his day.

It may have raised the moral tone of the educated classes that would listen, and resisted the immorality and rationalistic disbelief of what Cragg calls a 'hard-bitten society', but it was preached indiscriminately to the rustic and the industrial poor. 'Evil and guilt, and sin and redemption—the whole personal drama and appeal of religion—was forgotten, or rationalized away . . . it was not a religion which had much appeal to the men and women living brutal and squalid lives in the disease-ridden slums of the new towns and mining villages. They needed revelation and salvation.'[9]

It was against this background that Wesley and Whitefield preached. It may be sufficient indication of the change they brought into the pulpit, to note that Wesley's portrait of the 'Almost Christian' would almost fit Tillotson's ideal: 'The Almost Christian does nothing which the gospel forbids. He taketh not the name of God in vain . . . He profanes not the day of the Lord . . . He refrains from detraction, backbiting, talebearing, evil speaking . . . He avoids, as much as in him lies, all strife and contention . . . He uses the means of grace, yea all of them, at all opportunities. He constantly frequents the house of God . . .' Wesley goes on to say: 'The greatest question of all, then remains, Is the love of God shed abroad in your heart? Can you cry 'My God, my All? ... dost thou believe that Christ loved thee, and gave Himself for thee? Believest thou that the Lamb of God hath taken away thy sins, and cast them as a stone into the depth of the sea?'

Wesley and Whitefield replaced the prudential code with the saving cross. The point of division between them lay in the question of predestination. Whitefield took a firm Calvinistic stand, while Wesley preached salvation for all. Putting that difference on one side, it is possible to link the two together in their approach to the individual. The English poor in town and country had few rights and a great many hardships. Their future lay in the hands of their employers, who were very often the magistrates who administered justice. Food was scarce, prices were high, conditions of work degrading. Wesley offered them hope for the eternal future, which helped them tolerate the present; he gave them a new dignity as people known and loved by God. To the Christians of the middle and upper classes, who were dissatisfied with the dull formality of the Parish pulpit, Wesley demonstrated the living God, whose Spirit was at work in the hearts of men. Tillotson's God admitted to heaven those who had adequately fulfilled the conditions; Wesley's God, by an astounding act of grace, forgave the sinner.

In speaking to people as individuals Wesley spoke to a deep human need, passed by in the generalities of parochial preaching. '... there was an edge to life in the eighteenth century which is hard for us to recapture. In every class there is the same taut neurotic quality—the fantastic gambling and drinking, the riots, brutality and violence, and everywhere and always a constant sense of death . . . Methodism gave far more than emotional release; it brought a sense of purpose and a field for the exercise of both will and power.'[10]

The violence and harshness of medieval life had not entirely disappeared from the lives of the masses, and the preaching too had its medieval echoes, particularly in its lurid descriptions of hell and the fate of sinners. Whitefield was especially renowned in this respect, a contemporary writing of him:

> *He knows his Master's realm so well,*
> *His sermons are a map of Hell,*
> *An Ollio made of Conflagration,*
> *Of Gulphs of Brimstone and Damnation,*
> *Eternal Torments, Furnace, Worm . . .*

The evangelical preachers also gave the offer of salvation, and their preaching covered issues of practical Christian living, or religious observance, and the central truths of the Christian Faith, as a glance down the titles in the collections of Wesley's sermons quickly indicates.

The sung, as well as the spoken, word was also one of the media through which the Gospel was made known. Perhaps the hymns did for the eighteenth century crowds what the Mass and the religious festivals did for their medieval brethren, for many of them too were non-literate, but well able to commit verse to memory.

Wesley and Whitefield lived in a period of great educational and cultural contrasts. If their preaching was at times deficient in its intellectual appeal, or not sufficiently thorough-going in the development of its social and political implications, if a slightly superstitious belief in witches and devils persisted within it; it is only evidence that they were men of their age. The shape of the Gospel in their hands was determined by the needs of the people as they saw them, and the limitations imposed by the presuppositions of the age.

The Last Hundred Years

The tradition of Tillotson did not entirely disappear, and in any case much of the fire of early Methodist preaching died down within a few years of Wesley's death. The nineteenth century opened with a continuing legacy of arid moralizing, but a revitalization of preaching was coming, particularly during the second half of the century, springing from all parts of the Church. It was the result not simply of reaction against unsatisfying preaching as such, but because the period was one of intellectual turmoil, particularly over the origins of the universe through the work of Laplace, and the origin of man himself, through the work of Darwin. In the life of the Church the work of biblical criticism seemed to threaten the very core of authority. 'In such times, as the older stabilities are giving way, men seek guidance from their religious mentors and, if this is forthcoming, the churches and chapels will be crowded.'[11]

And it was forthcoming. Preachers who did not

57

evade the current issues, or offered refuge from them, found large audiences. In the main they took one of two approaches: either they maintained the old beliefs despite contemporary discoveries and theories, or they adopted the liberal approach of trying to synthesize the new knowledge and the old faith. Examples of the first approach can be found in the Baptist, C. H. Spurgeon, and in the Anglican, turned Roman Catholic, Cardinal J. H. Newman.

Spurgeon's appeal was mainly with the lower middle classes and manual workers. They heard him in their thousands, coming to him '. . . for new hope in the grinding struggle against poverty and temptation, to hear a man of the people who was also a man of God'.[12] He was a Calvinist in Whitefield's mould, and a fundamentalist. This gave his preaching an authority attractive to the unsophisticated. The 'new hope' lay in the dogmatic assertion of the inerrancy of Scripture, of the certainties of predestination, of the doctrine of justification by grace through faith. It was preached loudly, confidently, amusingly, colourfully. It appealed enormously to the heart, but never took seriously or sensitively the conscientious and perplexing questionings of the thinking Christians. 'That is an heroic faith which believes Christ in the teeth of a thousand contradictions. When the Lord gives you that faith, you can say, "I consult not with flesh and blood. He who said to me, 'Believe and be saved' gave me grace to believe, and therefore I am confident that I am saved. When once I cast my soul, sink or swim, upon the love, and blood, and power of Christ, though conscience give no witness to my soul, though doubts

distress me, and fears plague me, yet it is mine to honour my Master by believing his Word, though it be
contradictory to sense, though reason rebel against it,
and present feeling dare to give it the lie" ' (from the
sermon on John 4 : 48, 'The Marks of Faith').

If Spurgeon recalled men and women to Christ in
the Bible, Newman recalled them to Christ in the
Church. The whole man, intellect, will and spirit, must
be subservient to God in Christ. God has demonstrated his claim to man's allegiance through the Incarnation, Cross and Resurrection; He has given the
saints, as great examples, who '. . . track out for us the
way that leads heavenwards,' and Christ himself has
remained within the Church, and is physically present
in every Eucharist. The Church has direct continuity
with the Incarnation. These are the certainties to hold
on to in an age of scepticism.

By vastly different methods both Spurgeon and
Newman effectively preached Christ to their generation, and they preached religious conservatism appropriate to their respective traditions. In the face of
the changing and uncertain world they offered the
hope of heaven, although the paths thereto were poles
apart. They stood against the prevailing tendencies to
concentrate on the material world, and make scientific
method the new dogmatism.

The second approach, that of accepting the world as
science was making it known, and trying to understand the Christian faith within its context, can be seen
in the preaching of F. W. Robertson of Brighton, and
R. W. Dale of Birmingham.

Owen Chadwick[13] describes Robertson as a 'soul

battered by contending forces'. He did not in his own person radiate the sanctified composure of Newman or the confidence of Spurgeon. He was concerned with truth and wholeness in terms of a man's total response individually and corporately, and also in terms of the whole creation. Christ is the head of all creation, as well as of all men, and therefore no truth in science or history can contradict the Christian faith. His awareness of the questions raised by contemporary enquiry, and the obligation of the Christian to face them, is indicated by a reference in his sermon on 'The Scepticism of Pilate' to 'That priestly bigotry which forbids enquiry and makes doubt a crime'.[14]

At the heart of Robertson's preaching is the Incarnation. It is his historical grounding, and he exhorts those who could not conceive the divinity of Christ to first come to know him as a man, to feel with him, and walk with him through his earthly life: 'Live with Him until He becomes a living thought, ever present, and you will find a reverence growing up which compares with nothing else in all human experience.'[15]

'Experience' is one of Robertson's cornerstones. In living with Christ one comes to experience his divinity, in obeying God 'till the absolute imperative within you speaks' you will not just think God exists, you will know. This approach to faith makes it possible to be open to all the new discoveries and insights of the day, for 'no science can sweep away the everlasting love which the intellect does not even pretend to judge or recognize'.[16] The obvious dangers of such subjectivity are safeguarded by the constant historic reference to Jesus, and the far-reaching ethical implications of the

Gospel, for the individual and for society. Those
social implications are well dealt with in his sermons,
in which he sees the temptations of poverty as well as
the temptations of wealth, but uncompromisingly as-
serts the obligation to redress the injustices done to the
poor.

Dale, like Robertson, believed that experience was
the way to knowledge of God, and he too emphasized
the historic humanity of Jesus. This gave Christians
their immovable ground for faith, and the base from
which they could not ignore or evade the realities of
the contemporary world, but could face them and
become involved with them.

His early sermons were doctrinal, but he began to
feel that his task was not only to inform the mind but
to activate the will. The Christian's obligation was to
serve God in the world. He was to fight sin in the
world, for it pervaded all social relationships; he was
to work out his obedience in a worldly context. Dale
attempted to destroy the distinction between sacred
and secular. There was no specifically 'Christian'
vocation, but one could be equally called of God to be
an engineer, a tailor or a magistrate. This was a doctrine of vocation highly relevant to the industrialists
and tradesmen of Birmingham.

His most famous sermon was on 'Christian
Worldliness', and it was a grand assertion that this is
God's world. Otherworldliness is basically ingratitude
to God the Creator. In driving his hearers to set their
service to God in the context of their total environment, and encouraging full participation in politics
and local government, he was not trying to set up a

Christian political party, but rather to encourage individual Christians to be socially and politically responsible. However, he did try to bring a social cohesion in Christ by encouraging Christians of all occupations to think of themselves 'as comrades in a great army, fighting side by side, under the high command of God, against want, ignorance, disorder and sin'.[17]

Although only the merest glance has been taken, it is clear that there was great variety in Victorian preaching, most of it being a particular response to the pressures of the age. The social inequalities evoked, from those who were awake to them, the social gospel of Robertson and Dale, and men like F. D. Maurice, Charles Kingsley, and Hugh Price Hughes; it evoked from those who experienced them a positive reaction to the preaching of Spurgeon and men like D. L. Moody. Thoughtful men and women, looking for guidelines in an age of contrasts, change and intellectual upheaval, were attracted to men like Robertson or Newman. Although each man centred his preaching in Christ, and sought to win his hearers to his allegiance, the good news they saw emanating from him for their generation had for each a different expression.

And what of our century?

Perhaps because we are closer to it, the twentieth century seems much more complex than any other. Decreasing church attendance is an indication of the increasing secularization of society, while the intellectual attack on Christianity comes strongly from many quarters: philosophy, science, medicine, psychology. The potentiality for mankind's self-destruction, the rapidly increasing range of scientific and technical capability, the speed of communication, the mobility and affluence of our society, all bring their pressures, their confrontation with other patterns of thought and ways of life, their opportunity for diversion and escape from fundamental questions of life and meaning. The mass media, with their thirst for news, sensation and novelty, tend to produce superficial judgement of major questions, from which they fly away as soon as they have lighted on them. These are just a few random examples of the complex influences affecting the social climate in which the Gospel is to be proclaimed.

Within this environment the Church has had to reassess the content of its preaching, and its method; and to look closely at its own life and worship. The second concern is not unrelated to the first, and finds expression in the Ecumenical Movement, the Liturgical Movement, and the intensity and diversity of theological study and debate. These in their turn have affected the preaching of the Church.

Horton Davies in *Varieties of English Preaching, 1900-1960* suggests four basic types of preaching characteristic of the first half of the twentieth century: apologetic, expository, charismatic and liturgical. The existence of these different types illustrates the continuing effort of the Church to find the most relevant way of communicating its central truths in a changing and varied environment.

One is tempted to write off the charismatic as a definable type of preaching. The implication is that its appeal is as much to do with the personalities of the preachers as with the content of the preaching. The examples given are 'Dick' Sheppard and Studdert Kennedy. However, with them it was more than just having attractive personalities. They addressed the disillusion following the First World War, when people would no longer be satisfied with the distant bland God of the conventional clergyman. Through these two men thousands came to see God as one who understood and shared their suffering and anguish, who was with them in their daily lives. If it is true that it was in the lives of these men themselves that people saw, in symbol, the living, serving, truly sympathetic God, then it may not tell us much about the structure of their proclamation, but it points to lessons which most preachers and the Church itself have yet to learn.

Liturgical preaching, exemplified in Davies by Ronald Knox, is preaching set within the context of worship, disciplined by lectionary and calendar. It is one of the fruits of the Liturgical Movement, and we shall look at it again in the conclusion to this article.

In a way, expository preaching is like liturgical preaching. It stems directly from the Bible, and is aimed at making the word of God in scripture become the living Word of God in contemporary life. Ethical, apologetic, evangelistic, topical sermons can all arise from expository preaching. (The wide range of topics covered by Dr Sangster and Dr Weatherhead bears this out.) It is significant in our era, because it represents a longing for authority in an age of mobile uncertainties. The popularity of some very conservative evangelical preachers is evidence of this.

The apologetic preaching of this century aims

'... to remove the errors that stand as barriers to belief, whether these be intellectual, moral or psychological.'[18] It attempts to show that faith and reason do not contradict one another, and that Christianity is relevant to the needs of men and society. Preaching of this type was inevitable unless the Church was to be deaf to the questions and insensitive to the pressures of modern life. To pick out common characteristics of the sermons preached by the great number of people who have taken up this challenge is difficult. Some, like Tillich, have tried to pin-point the deepest, unconscious longings and fears of men and women, as in his sermons in *The Shaking of the Foundations* and especially in the magnificent 'You are Accepted'; and, in the offer of Christ to meet those longings and fears, has opened the way for people to experience the reality of God. 'Grace strikes us when we are in great pain and restlessness. It strikes us when we walk through the dark valley of meaninglessness and empty life. It strikes us when we feel that our separation is deeper than usual, because we have violated another life, a life which we loved, or from which we were estranged. It strikes us when our disgust for our own being, our indifference, our weakness, our hostility, and lack of direction and composure have become intolerable to us.... Sometimes at that moment a wave of light breaks into our darkness, and it is as though a voice were saying: "You are accepted. *You are accepted*, accepted by that which is greater than you, and the name of which you do not know. Do not ask for the name now; perhaps you will find it later. Do not try to do anything now; perhaps later you will do much. Do not seek for anything; do not perform anything; do not intend anything. *Simply accept the fact that you are accepted!*" If that happens to us, we experience grace.'[19] Others, like H. H. Farmer, who at times shares Tillich's approach, have taken up the depersonalizing effect of much of industry and urban life, and the prevalent sense of futility, and presented the individual with the personal love of Christ within an eternal purpose. These men back their preaching with profound scholarship which has commanded the respect of Christian and atheist alike. Yet others, like Leonard Griffith, have systematically taken up the common 'Barriers to Belief' such as suffering and the problem of evil, and dealt with them directly.

Despite vast differences in style and approach, the world-asserting implication of the Incarnation is certainly a common foundation for twentieth-century apologetic preaching. The world is the sphere of God's activity, within that world people matter to God, and their needs, questions and concerns are treated by these preachers with the utmost seriousness, for, to them, man in his entirety must come within the 'sphere of God's grace'.

Conclusion

When we look back at the shape of the Gospel in history we can see marked changes from age to age, and variety within each generation. If it is true that 'How the fact of God in Christ is to be seen as good news depends upon the needs and conditions of the time' (page 46), then that is to be expected. The Church has the responsibility to preserve its essential Christocentric message and make it known in ways that each succeeding generation, and all the varied elements within them, can understand, and it has—as this essay has perhaps shown—been more successful in doing this in some generations than in others. To think that there is a universal formula in which the Gospel can be expressed in every generation, and that is how the 'true Gospel' has been preached from the time of the Apostles, is simply not true.

It also needs to be noted that the responsibility for evangelism is laid upon the whole Church, not just the preachers within it. The preacher must ask where else, in the life of the Church, God's good news for our generation is made known, and set his or her preaching within the context of the whole of the Church's life. This is the importance of liturgical preaching, which in many cases may direct the hearers to other aspects of the Church's work and worship through which God will speak to them. Tillich's theme of 'You are accepted' for instance, can be taken up through the accepting fellowship of the Church, or through the Eucharist. In fact, if people cannot find confirmation of the spoken word in the life of the Church almost all of preaching's effectiveness is dissipated.

One of the lessons of history is that preaching cannot be treated in isolation, that the Gospel is given to the whole Church to exemplify and proclaim in each generation. So we must ask what the Gospel is for our generation, and how the Church can most effectively proclaim it. These very relevant questions are taken up in other parts of this book.

Preacher's Handbook

NOTES

1. cf. *The Apostolic Preaching and its Developments.*
2. G. R. Owst, *Preaching in Medieval England,* p. 338.
3. Op. cit., pp. 336-7.
4. Op. cit., p. 201.
5. Op. cit., p. 243.
6. Ibid.
7. Bishop Burnet, q. *Chambers's Biographical Dictionary.*
8. *The Church and the Age of Reason,* p. 80.
9. J. H. Plumb, *England in the 18th Century,* pp. 44-5.
10. Op. cit., p. 95.
11. H. Davies, *Worship and Theology in England,* Vol. 4, p. 282.
12. Op. cit., p. 343.
13. *The Victorian Church,* Vol. 2, p. 135.
14. cf. C. Smyth, *The Art of Preaching 747-1939,* p. 39.
15. H. Davies, *Worship and Theology in England,* Vol. 4, p. 316.
16. Op. cit., p. 317.
17. Op. cit., p. 328.
18. Op. cit., Vol. 5, p. 212.
19. *The Shaking of the Foundations* (Penguin ed.), p. 163.

BOOKS

The Apostolic Preaching and its Developments—C. H. Dodd (Hodder & Stoughton)
Preaching in Medieval England—G. R. Owst (Cambridge University Press)
Pulpit and Literature in Medieval England—G. R. Owst (Blackwell)
The Church and the Age of Reason—G. R. Cragg (Pelican)
The Church in an Age of Revolution—A. R. Vidler (Pelican)
The Art of Preaching 747-1939—Charles Smyth (SCM Press)
Worship and Theology in England—Horton Davies (5 vols.) (SCM Press)
Varieties of English Preaching 1900-1960—Horton Davies (SCM Press)
The Eighteenth-Century Pulpit—James Downey (Oxford University Press)
Sermons and Society—ed. Paul A. Welsby (Pelican)

68

The Gospel for Today

Pauline M. Webb

AT A QUARTER to two in the afternoon of 25th January, 1946, in the chapel of King's College, London, I became a committed Christian. At that moment the message of Christ was for me an intensely personal, deeply spiritual, purely private message of love. In responding to that love at last I experienced an exhilarating sense of liberation. After months of debating in my head, I had now grasped the truth with my heart, after a long struggle of obsession with myself about what I wanted to become, I could now, by God's grace, just let myself be. I didn't know how to put it into words. This was the kind of experience you can only sing about. Charles Wesley had done that for me:

> *My chains fell off, my heart was free,*
> *I rose, went forth, and followed Thee.*

Twenty-five years later, at a quarter to two in the afternoon of 25th January, 1971, I sat in Jan Smuts airport in Johannesburg, waiting to know what the authorities would do with me. They had refused me entry to their country, presumably because of my connection with the World Council of Churches and the recent action of that body in aiding liberation movements in Southern Africa. As I waited, alone, thinking back over that experience of twenty-five years before, I suddenly realized how all this was part of that very same commitment. The words I had sung then to express a gospel I had received in personal, spiritual terms were equally relevant now to a commitment that had come to have corporate, political, even international significance. This gospel is good news about liberation—liberation for each man and liberation for all men; liberation from all that would keep me from my full destiny as a child of God, and liberation from all that would prevent all men from realizing their full dignity as the heirs of Christ. This is the good news this Son of Man came to bring—good news for poor and hungry people who are to be filled with good things; good news for imprisoned and oppressed people who are to be set free; good news for blind people who are to recover their sight; good news for us all, sinners as we are, who are to discover that even so we are loved and that in the here and now, in this present moment, we can know what it is to live in the Lord's favour.

To take the words of the gospel literally, to let them speak to us plainly without gloss or specially spiritualized interpretation, can be a shocking experience. I find St Luke's account of the gospel the plainest and most straightforward. Emphasizing as it does both the personal and the universal good news that Jesus came to bring, this gospel reads at times like a subversive pamphlet of some revolutionary movement. Again and again it resounds with the message of liberation. Man, and woman too, is to be set free—free from all that enslaves the body or the soul, alone and in community. Here is a message so startlingly relevant to man's search in our own time that it is not surprising that there are parts of the world where the Bible is a banned book and where preaching the gospel is regarded as a potentially dangerous political activity. But so it has always been. Men have tried to fetter this book in chains, to wrap its words up in mystery, to shut away its preachers in remote pulpits in archaic buildings, to express its message in the language of some other day and some other culture lest the people hear with their ears and understand these words in the present tense! Perhaps the most important task a modern preacher has to do is to let the Word of God speak itself in the language of men today. And to do that, we need to know the language, the longings and aspirations of our contemporary society. Whenever one wishes to interpret a message to people of another tongue or culture, it is the messenger who must do the work of learning the new language, not the other way round. So often we preachers seem to require of people that they shall first learn the terminology of the Christian Church and understand the aspirations and concepts of the people of Israel before they can even hear what the good news is. It is we who need to do the job of translating our traditional Christian terminology into the language of today and of recognizing how, underlying the Judaic connotations of the Biblical message, are the hopes and fears, the aspirations and despairs of contemporary and universal man.

Let us then try to hear the gospel for today coming to us through the gospel of St Luke. We begin at the beginning, with the stories of the birth of Jesus. It all begins when a young woman says 'Yes' to the purpose of God for her life and for the life of all mankind. She cannot possibly understand fully what that purpose is. It does not accord at all with her own plans for herself. But Mary's 'Yes' is required to make possible the coming of a Saviour to the world. Today a 'Yes', an affirmation, an acceptance, a readiness to embrace life and not draw away from it, is required of us if we are to be bearers of faith, of hope, of love in a world which is looking desperately for the means of its salvation. The Christian is one who never despairs of the world—because of his astonishing faith that both he himself and the whole world are loved, are caught up in one great purpose of good, and that to co-operate with that purpose, however and wherever it might lead us, is to share an intimate relationship with God himself. Dag Hammersjöld, that man who, as General Secretary of the United Nations, spent his life striving for international peace and universal justice, describes his own personal motivation in terms of saying 'Yes'. Writing of a conversion experience on Whitsunday 1961, he says: 'I don't know who or what put the question, I don't know when it was put. I don't even remember answering. But at some moment I did answer Yes to Someone or Something and from that hour I was certain that existence is meaningful, and that therefore my life is self-surrender, had a goal.'

To be certain that existence is meaningful is a profound need for modern man, whose temptation is to treat it as absurd, 'a tale told by an idiot . . . signifying nothing', or as cheap, to be thrown on to the rubbish dump of a slum or slaughtered on a battlefield, or downright evil, locked in powers bent on destruction. The good news of the coming of Christ is news that God takes man so seriously that he shares his life, that the divine has a human face; it is news that God values man so highly that he has set an incalculable price upon his head so that to rob man of his dignity is to rob God himself of his life-blood; it is news that the powers of good are always ultimately stronger than the powers of evil and that every commitment to the search for justice (so often translated in the Bible as 'righteousness'), peace (which in the Bible is seen to include the well-being of the whole community), truth (better translated 'trust' or faithfulness) is a participation in the very purpose of God. Our obedience in such participation is required if men are to see that Jesus, the Saviour (the Liberator is an equally valid translation), is come into the World.

No wonder that when Mary grasps the part that she is to play in enabling the purpose of God to be fulfilled, she bursts into song—a song of liberation. I remember once being in St Paul's Cathedral in the presence of the royal family, where, after solemn procession in dignified robes, the choir, in perfect harmony, chanted the Magnificat. And quite suddenly, beautiful though the majesty of the occasion was, it struck me as utterly incongruous. Read again the words of that ancient song (Luke 1:46-55) in a modern translation and one feels that the right setting for it is anywhere but an ancient cathedral and a royal occasion. Rather it belongs to the world's battlefield where men are fighting for their dignity and liberty—whether that battlefield be the war on want, the struggle for social justice, the campaign for political freedom or the crusade against all that exploits, debases or diminishes the life of men. For God has 'magnified' man, he has called into being a new universal humanity, he has turned the normal values of the world upside down, so that those who set themselves up as great are humbled before him and the little people of the earth discover that he is on their side. So Mary recalls the story of Abraham in whom 'all the families of the earth will be blessed' (Genesis 12:3) and the birth of her Son is seen to have universal significance.

The same message of liberation is taken up by Zechariah when he greets the birth of his own son, the prophet John, the one chosen to prepare the way for the coming of the Liberator. He sees the child in the direct line of succession of those men who in every age have been raised up by God to challenge the enemies of his people, to scrutinize the justice of their rulers and to ensure that men shall have a free, full, abundant life, fulfilling the very purpose of their creation.

There is the sense throughout the Bible that the joys of creation, the acclamation of the whole created universe, accompany every effort of man to share in the work of creating a better world. Creation itself is the work of Jesus and the work of man. It has been put into man's hands, to develop the world and all its resources or to destroy it. And that development of the world requires a commitment to just dealings with men. Zechariah quotes King David as the symbol of such commitment, recalling the magnificent phrases of 2 Samuel 23:3-4 (NEB):

'He who makes men in justice
Who rules in the fear of God,
is like the light of morning at sunrise,
a morning that is cloudless after rain
and makes the grass sparkle from the earth.'

Again, a modern writer has echoed this positive affirmation of life and of God's creation which heralds the coming of Jesus. E. E. Cummings, exulting in the glory of a new-born day, catches something of the sheer joy of Zechariah's song:

i thank you God for this most amazing
day: for the leaping greenly spirits of trees
and a blue true dream of sky; and for everything
which is natural, which is infinite, which is yes
i who have died am alive again today
and this is the sun's birthday; this is the birth
day of life and of love and wings, and of the gay
great happening illimitably earth.

So Jesus is come into the world. The good news is told to the men out in the fields, minding their sheep. It is *good* news, of *great* joy for *all* people. A deliverer, a liberator, has come. It is workmen, not wise men, who first hear the announcement in Luke's account. To the workman the Christ is announced in the midst of his work, in the carrying out of his routine tasks. Out on a cold night on the hills, in the taxing conditions under which herdsmen still live in so many parts of the world, the shepherds see the splendour of the Lord. Here would be good news indeed—that men might be released from drudgery and from the sordid conditions under which so many of them labour, to enjoy the sheer splendour of living and to see glory shining round about them. Every man has the right to work, as part of his very fulfilment as a man, but no man's work should be allowed so to demean him that he can no longer see the glory of life even on his own hillside. For God's favour rests upon men and his good will is for their well-being, whoever they might be and whatever the work they do.

One of the positive things about the age in which we live is that man can be freed from so much of the drudgery of life—but this will mean nothing unless he is enabled too to enjoy its glory. The increased leisure that modern technology promises to us could be as soul-destroying as constant toil if it does not enable men to open their ears and their eyes to the music and poetry and splendour of life all around them, to discover that they are indeed people liberated by the One who has come 'that they might have life and have it more abundantly.'

Even the old people, the ones who had waited long and faithfully for the liberation of their country, see at last in the coming of Jesus the coming of that liberation. Simeon's *Nunc Dimittis* (Luke 2:29-32) recalls the great promise of the prophet in Isaiah 49—a passage which for me recently suddenly leapt into almost overwhelmingly powerful relevance when I read it for the opening devotions of a meeting called to discuss the responsibilities of Christians in combating racism. Some of our group were men exiled from their own land because of their demands for racial equality and I sensed the quickening of their pulses as they heard again the promises of God:

> 'Thus says the Holy one,
> to one who thinks little of himself,
> whom every nation abhors,
> the slave of tyrants. . . .
> In the hour of my favour I answered you
> and I helped you on the day of deliverance,
> putting the land to rights
> and sharing out afresh its desolate fields;
> I said to the prisoners, "Go free"
> and to those in darkness, "Come out and be
> seen".'
>
> (Isaiah 49:7-8.)

It is this promise of liberation for the people of Israel which Simeon sees as a sign for all nations. But the accomplishment of such liberation is no tea-party. In Luke 2:34-5 we are reminded that conflict and suffering and exposure of the real human situation will accompany the arrival on the scene of the Liberator. We must never expect the Gospel to have an easy passage.

There is a tradition that Luke's gospel was written from the memories of the women who knew Jesus. Certainly his mother figures prominently in these early chapters and her longings for her son are deeply expressed. But even in these early years she has to learn the lesson of a love that liberates rather than imprisons. She learns that to love someone means not only to give them life, but also to set them free. 'Love them and let them be' is wise counsel to any mother concerning her children. Yet setting free never means cutting off. Simeon reminds Mary that love means sharing suffering (Luke 2:25). To love someone is to be doubly vulnerable—not only to the hurt one suffers oneself but also to the hurts suffered by the one who is loved. Watch any mother sitting by the bedside of her sick child and you see the pain written on her face as deeply as it is on his. The sword that pierced Jesus' side pierced the heart of his mother standing at the Cross. Yet, in the strange mystery of love, that very sharing of suffering liberates us from its power. Is this human experience of love not a help to our understanding of what it means to say of Jesus 'Surely he has borne our griefs and carried our sorrows—and by his stripes we are healed'? (Isaiah 53:4-5). It is his love that saves us, not his suffering. His love gives us life, his love sets us free, his love takes away our hurt.

In contrast to the tenderness of Mary's love, Luke shows us in these early chapters of his gospel the strong anger of John the Baptist. Sometimes when I have been confronted by people smarting with a sense of injustice so raw that they have flayed about them in intense indignation, in vehement language, in violent action, I have been tempted to dismiss them as hysterical extremists and so shut my ears to the words of judgement their anger might well be speaking against me and my kind and the society which has made us. None of the Black Power agitators, the Shelter squatters, the student demonstrators could be more offensive in manner than John the Baptist must have been to the self-righteous Jews of his day. He reminds them of what repentance really means—a change from self-righteousness to a concern for righteousness (justice) for all mankind. He puts his demands in very practical terms—fair shares, no exploitation, no bullying, (Luke 3:13-14). This is the kind of repentance that will make possible the good news of man's liberation.

But before that good news is fully spelt out, Jesus himself needs time to work out how best it is to be communicated to men. In the temptations in the wilderness (Luke 4:1-13) he rejects the normal approach to dealing with human affairs—the current Roman practice of bread and circuses. He goes rather to the roots of the matter. God's word recognizes not solely man's physical nature and need, but his whole humanity and dignity; to take God seriously as ruler of the world is to be unable to take any other powers with ultimate unquestioning seriousness; to express solidarity with suffering mankind precludes any cheap reliance on supernatural protection. Man must take full responsibility for his own actions and even for the sufferings they might cause, so that man might be truly free.

So, Luke has set the stage for the great proclamation of the good news of liberation announced by Jesus in his own local synagogue in terms so plain that his congregation could not miss his meaning. At first they smile benignly at his safe reading of the Scriptures—its words have become blunted by familiarity—but then he drives his point home to them—here and now in their own home town— reminding them that they cannot bask in any special favour, that this good news of liberation is meant for all mankind and indeed many foreigners have proved to be more worthy of its benefits than the chosen people of Israel. No wonder they threw him out of the synagogue. This was dangerously controversial material with political connotations. Non-patrials enjoying benefits denied to those who have Abraham for their father! The only people to whom this would have sounded like good news were probably excluded from the synagogue altogether!

From then on the first part of Luke's gospel tells us stories which at first demonstrate what this liberation means for the victims—in physical terms, it is a fight against all disease that diminishes man's life. Jesus never accepted sickness or deformity as 'the will of God'. And neither must we. All suffering, whether it be that caused by nature or that caused by man against his fellow-man, must be resisted in the name of Christ. The sick man must struggle with all his might against his sickness; the oppressed man must struggle against oppression. And in this struggle is released an extraordinary energy—there is a power available in which the physician who strives to heal can put his trust; there is a power available on which the politician who struggles for justice can pin his faith; there is a power available in which every inhibited, paralysed human soul can find meaning for his life as he opens up himself to love and knows his sins forgiven.

Among the many healing stories, one of the most significant for our theme of liberation is that in Luke 6:6-10. The Sabbath had originally been the day on which the Jewish people celebrated their liberation from slavery. But now the rules regulating such celebration had made the very day itself a bondage. So Jesus comes into open confrontation with the religious authorities. He could presumably have equally easily healed the man's withered arm on a Monday, but he wants to challenge their understanding of what this 'holy' day is all about, if it is not about 'healing' (Note the close connection between the two words). He asks them the straight question—'Is it more important to save life or to destroy it?' This is surely the question to ask in a permissive society like ours. Not 'Does this or that action obey the rules?' but 'Does it enrich or diminish life, ennoble or demean it, create or destroy?'

Mark's account of the story (Mark 3:4) says that the religious leaders had nothing to say—they were silent in answer to such a fundamental question. And Jesus was filled with 'anger and sorrow at their obstinate stupidity'. The silence of religious men in face of human suffering must make him angry still.

What Jesus says (see the very literal words of

Luke's account of the Sermon on the Mount in Luke 6) is always demonstrated by what he does. So when John the Baptist's disciples send to know his credentials he can only reply in terms not of his preaching but of his programme, his acts of liberating men from all the sordid things which enslave or limit their existence (Luke 7:22-3). Would that we, as we try to communicate the good news today, had a like catalogue of deeds done in his name that would demonstrate that we really do mean what we say! For this is the age in which quite literally many of the works that Jesus did we can do too, and greater works than these. The healing of leprosy, the feeding of the hungry, the restoring of dignity to the poor, the enrichment of the whole of life for all men in this world are possibilities within our grasp.

How can the victims of man's inhumanity to man ever hear the good news of the humanity of God unless they see the works of God—the healing, feeding, loving, forgiving, liberating work of God being done amongst them, made all the more possible by the liberated power and energy God has entrusted to man's hand? It will be no dramatic 'Deus ex machina' act which will bring in the Kingdom, nor a proclamation of doom against the world and the promise of pie in the sky for the favoured. It is in the here and now, through the acts of men that we shall discover the Christ come among us.

One 'liberation' idea that receives little serious attention from most Christian pulpits is the contemporary one of the liberation of women. Yet this too is an expression of the good news of the coming of Jesus. Dorothy Sayers in her witty and searching essay 'The Human not quite Human', writes of Jesus' own attitude: 'Perhaps it is no wonder that the women were first at the cradle and last at the Cross. They had never known a man like this Man—a prophet and teacher who never nagged at them, never flattered or coaxed or patronised; who never made arch jokes about them, never treated them either as "The women, God help us!" or "The ladies, God bless them!", who rebuked without querulousness and praised without condescension; who took their questions and arguments seriously; who never mapped out their sphere for them, never urged them to be feminine or jeered at them for being female; who had no axe to grind and no uneasy male dignity to defend; who took them as he found them and was completely unself-conscious.'

Particularly is this graciousness, this liberating quality shown in Luke's account of the woman who anointed Jesus' feet in the house of Simon the leper (Luke 7:36-50). The story ends with words that can be translated 'Your trust has liberated you'. The woman trusted Jesus to understand the intention of her love—to see her not as other men saw, as a body to be enjoyed, but to recognize her as a whole person longing for a truly free and human existence. Her freedom was constantly denied by the demands men made upon her, even the price they paid for her favours. She wanted to give, in love, for love to a woman is a total relationship, not a momentary satisfaction. When love is bought or bargained over it is cheapened and degrading. But given freely and joyfully to one who understands the meaning of the gift it becomes an enriching, ennobling experience in which this woman finds her own soul. 'Go in peace', says Jesus—in that extravagant sharing of love which shows that you yourself have received love great enough to forgive all your sins.

Constantly, throughout this gospel, Jesus is enlarging his disciples' understanding of the limitless outreachings of love. He will not even allow 'kith or kin' to be given a priority place in his responsibilities (Luke 8:19-21). No family, tribal, national or racial ties must proscribe the limits of our concern for men's liberation. Not even economic considerations can be allowed to be a determining factor. In the healing of Legion, in the Gadarene countryside, (Luke 8:26-39) Jesus is far more concerned about the man and his need to be liberated from the forces that possess him than about the swine, which would represent the economic livelihood of the community. From that community this man had been excluded as one dead (living among the tombs) but now through his liberation he is re-integrated. Jesus insists that he live out that liberation not by going away but by staying in the community which has been so hostile to him.

Preachers of the gospel today face possibly their greatest opposition when what they say or do seems to threaten the economic interests of those to whom they minister. It is tempting to try to avoid such a clash, but if people are truly to be liberated, such a conflict is inevitable. Yet again and again we discover economic realities to be the acid test of a man's commitment. Where his treasure is, there will his heart be also. So Jesus warns his disciples, that they must be free from all interests that would become a bondage to them (Luke 9 : 1-6). There is only one commitment that a Christian is free to make, and that is the commitment to the way of the Cross (Luke 9 : 23-6). 'Hold fast to Christ', said Herbert J. Butterfield, 'and for the rest be totally uncommitted.' Today such words come with great force to a generation which suspects all commitment to any kind of institution to be a new form of bondage. To many young people today, commitment is expressed in doing the deed, in going on the march, in being where the action is—not in subscribing to a club or signing on the dotted line. And it is on the march—walking the Way of the Cross, not merely belonging to the Church, that we learn the meaning of commitment to Jesus. On this journey we may catch up with many fellow-pilgrims, those who walk this way even without naming the Name of the One we know as the Way. To those who have seen Christ transfigured before them (Luke 9 : 29-36) there can be no doubt who he is, though words fail us adequately to express our understanding. But down in the market-place, we find him among many who may not recognize him but who yet stand by his side (Luke 9 : 49-50).

One Sunday a couple of years ago I spent the Lord's day in an unusual place. It was in the Roundhouse, a large disused engine shed in Chalk Farm. It was an uglier building than the ugliest of all Methodist Central Halls. Nothing had been done to

make it comfortable. We were asked to sit there all
day from 9 a.m. to 9 p.m. and pay fifteen shillings for
the privilege! We were able to get only cheese and
rolls to eat. We had umpteen very long speeches to
listen to. Yet in that audience were over a thousand
young people—most of them would never be seen
dead in our redecorated, coffee-providing, shortened-
service, places of worship. Yet on that Sunday they
listened with greatest attention of all to a wizened
little archbishop whose credentials were that he has
been totally engaged in the struggle against poverty
in Brazil and who said to these young people, who
were there because they too wanted to engage more
actively in the fight against world hunger, 'I don't
care what you call yourselves, if you stand beside the
poor, the oppressed, the little peoples of this earth,
you are standing alongside Jesus who came to set
them free.' And Archbishop Hilda Camara received a
standing ovation from those to whom this was good
news indeed—the liberating force of the gospel.

It would be tempting to go on right through
Luke's gospel and through the growing conflict that
such a struggle inevitably involves, demonstrating
from almost every story that this gospel is good
news about the liberation of man—*from* the individual and corporate consequences of sin, *from* physical suffering and political oppression, *from* all
human bondage, and especially from death—a liberation which frees him *for* self-fulfilment through his
own self-offering, *for* responsibility and participation
in the unfinished work of creation, *for* life that liber-

ates him from death because of the ultimate triumph
and resurrection of love.

Yet as Luke's gospel continues, we come to see
that those who need liberating are not only the poor
and oppressed but also the rich and the oppressors.
We meet many more people in bondage—most of
them religious people—see the priest, the Levite,
(Luke 10:25-37), the Pharisees (Luke 11:37-54), the
rich man (Luke 12:13-21), Dives (Luke 16:19-31),
the younger and the elder brother (Luke 15:11-32),
the rich young ruler (Luke 18:18-30). All of these
too need liberating from themselves, a liberation
they can only experience by living for others. 'No
one is free who does not work for the freedom of
others', said Karl Jaspers.

So we reach the great liberating act into which
are gathered all the deeds and words of Jesus. Having gone into headlong confrontation with all the
powers that hold men in bondage, he himself is
bound by them—imprisoned in pain and physical
torment, tortured and mocked by oppressors and
oppressed alike, bound firm to a cross from which
he will not make escape, defeated by the threat of
death to silence him for ever, deserted even by his
faith that God himself shares his cause. He has
reached the ultimate in self-giving and finally in the
last moment he expresses his own total liberation by
freely and willingly committing himself into the
hand of his Father. So he dies, in faith, in hope and
in love. They seal up his body—but the very stone
rolls away and the liberating power brings him
triumphant from the grave. Faith, hope, love are

vindicated and are set free for all the world to share.

This is indeed good news for our day—for a world in which fear, despair, suspicion hold men in bondage still. All are looking for the liberation. How then today do we appropriate this good news of liberation? First by faith—by trust in this living Christ and through him learning to trust our fellow men; then by a hope which enables us to work and live for the promised future of a liberated, new humanity because Christ is known as its pioneer and he has already opened the way to it; and then by living fully in love, a love which transcends and traverses all human barriers of race, and class, and sex, and physical limitation and political circumstance and ultimately even death itself, and in that love we find our liberation.

The Universality of the Gospel

John H. S. Crossley

THE MISSION HOUSE in its wisdom had asked me to speak to a Rotary Club in East Anglia. From my Birmingham suburb I set out at 5.30 a.m. for my journey by bus, train, tube, train and bus, to reach the hotel in time for the Rotary lunch.

'A sticky wicket', someone had warned me. 'These Rotary chaps, wonderful humanitarians, full of good works—but you can't get them interested in religion and church.' I don't say the remark is true, but it was enough to make me nervous; and it is true that Rotary is by constitution non-sectarian, and not normally the place for a missionary deputation address. I was glad of a cup of coffee before the meeting.

The hospitality secretary welcomed me with charming courtesy—and opened the bowling. 'As a boy, I had to go to church three times on Sunday. We looked forward to Missionary Sunday. We wanted to see the curios the missionaries brought. But now I wonder. *Is it right to try to convert people of other races*?

Shouldn't we respect their religions as much as our own? . . .'

Then came the time for my speech. Let me start with the common ground, our humanitarian concern. What were those statistics I heard from Dr Souster? 'Last year, in hospitals and clinics around the world associated with the Methodist Missionary Society, 54 tons of babies were born. Or put it another way, enough babies to fill the Royal Albert Hall three times. Hundreds of thousands of people would have had no modern medical care and no education, but for the work of this Society. . . . Of course, I don't come to beat a drum for one denomination. Many other religious societies could give you similar reports. Increasingly we work in close co-operation with such great charities as Oxfam, Save the Children; increasingly governments do all they can.

'Yet man does not live by bread alone. Man needs food, health, education, yet even more important are spiritual values, the sense of right and wrong, compassion and justice. Some of us still dare to believe that it is Jesus Christ who shows the true values; that to follow him is to find the meaning of life.

'Now this is the big question mark over missionary work today. Here in Britain our whole culture and civilization has a Christian background, and most of you will agree that the Church is right to preach Jesus Christ here. But many people today ask, *"Should we try to convert men of other countries? Haven't they already got their own religions? Why should we impose ours on them? Aren't all religions basically the same? Do you really believe that the millions of*

Hindus, Sikhs, Muslims are going to hell just because they don't believe in your Jesus?" . . .'

They were a lively audience, and they rose to the topic. Questions came thick and fast. At the end someone confessed with a twinkle, 'I told my friend, "There's a person preaching a sermon today. We'd better stay at home." But I'm glad I came. I enjoyed it.'

The topic is vital. It catches the interest of those fine people outside or on the fringe of the Church. It's great for a sixth form. But more than that, it is basic for our own faith.

Is the Gospel universal? Is it God's supreme word for all mankind? Is Christ really 'Lord of all'? Or is Christianity only one of the various ways in which mankind finds spiritual comfort—but maybe Hinduism, or Islam, or humanism, is just as good for those who prefer it?

Is the Church, then, a sort of a religious club for those who are that way inclined? That is useful, but not so very important. Or are we the people to whom God has entrusted the secret of the world's salvation? Then we must be utterly dedicated, as the top athlete to his training or the Communist to his Party.

Let us have a closer look at the questions raised above about the Christian attitude to other faiths.

1. *Shouldn't we respect other religions*? Yes, we should! Sadly the misconception has grown up that we Christians must criticise and condemn other

religions, in order to prove that our own is better. On the contrary, the true Christian way is to be as generous as possible in our estimation of other religions and cultures, to look for the best and noblest in them. See how charitable Jesus was towards Gentiles and Samaritans; see his praise of the Centurion and of the Samaritan leper, his story of the good Samaritan (Matt 8 : 10-12; Luke 17 : 11-19; 10 : 29-37).

The Bible teaches us to acknowledge the work of God in non-Christians. Already in the Old Testament the pagan King Cyrus is, mysteriously, an instrument of God's salvation. According to Paul, the pagans have some kind of knowledge of God. Peter roundly declares, 'God treats all men alike. Whoever fears him and does what is right, is acceptable to him'—but more of this text later (Is 45 : 1-6; Ro 1 : 19-20; Ac 10 : 34-5).

Therefore, in all faithfulness to Christ, we can be eager to discern the work of God in Mahatma Gandhi, in U Thant, or in those good humanitarians among our friends. We can readily confess that men who do not know Christ often put us to shame with their Christ-likeness.

2. *Must we believe that all non-Christians are going to hell, unless they accept Christ?* Most Christians do not believe so. True, this was one of the great missionary motives of the nineteenth century, and it produced a marvellous zeal to take the Gospel to as many people as possible before they died. But most of us now find it incredible that God, as we know him in Christ,

should condemn people for not believing in one of whom they had never even heard. Nor does the Bible compel us to believe this.

Divine judgement is written indelibly into the Gospel story, and necessity is still laid upon us to proclaim the way of salvation in Jesus Christ. But Bible texts such as John 3:18, 'he who believes in him is not condemned; he who does not believe is condemned already, because he has not believed in the name of the only Son of God', must be read in their context. They apply only to those who, in God's sight, have had a fair chance of understanding and believing the Gospel. The Bible hints that God has his own way of judging those who never knew the Gospel (Ro 2:14-16); and Jesus warns against too much speculation on this subject. 'Are there few that are saved?' asked the disciples. 'See to yourself,' replied Jesus, 'see that *you* enter in by the narrow door' (Luke 13:23 f).

3. *Should we impose our religion on people of other cultures?* The answer to this is a plain *No*, but we must add that the questioner is out of date in his idea of missionary work. No doubt in the heyday of colonialism, Christianity was exported as part of the package of 'civilization' that the white races spread round the world. No doubt, also, there were sometimes inducements and pressures to accept Christianity.

But how the position has changed! Today, most of us white people are so afraid of 'imposing our religion' that we are quite inhibited from telling people about Christ. While on the contrary, in several non-Western cultures, indigenous churches are engaged in the most vigorous evangelism among their own peoples, with little or no missionary assistance. It's time we woke up to this fact—we live in one of the great ages of Christian expansion. In South America, in Africa, in Indonesia millions are turning to Christ. In the year 1900, 1 per cent of Africans (South of Sahara) were Christians. Today some 40 per cent profess to follow Christ. On present trends, there will, by 1990, be more professing Christians in Africa than in the whole of North America. So far from Christianity being imposed, the problem for the church in 'black Africa' is how to give adequate pastoral care to the masses who are already and spontaneously turning to call themselves Christians.

It is no part of Christian duty to force or bribe people to profess Christianity; still less, to impose on them the outward forms in which we express our faith. But it is authentically Christian to say, 'This news of Jesus Christ is so good, we must recommend it to all the world'.

Remembering these points, let us look at the religions—not to criticise and judge, but with sincere desire to understand. Some people say, 'All religions are the same'. With respect, this is simply nonsense. A glance at the religions reveals the quite astonishing diversity of their teachings. We often take it for granted that 'religion' is the worship of gods or of God. But one great stream of Buddhist thought denies the existence of any god at all. There is no

Creator, there is no one there to worship. If language has any meaning, this is not 'the same' as Christianity!

One can see how the misconception arises. Human nature is the same—everywhere man has the same experience of joy and sorrow, the same need for a sense of purpose, unity and discipline. Everywhere man expresses his aspirations in the form of religion, or of such semi-religions as Communism and nationalism. But what the religions teach as the answer to man's aspiration is strikingly different.

The 'great divide' among the religions is their attitude to the events of history. One great class of religions sees life as a wheel, rotating around a stationary point. Plants, animals, human beings and institutions go through the never-ending cycle of birth, growth, decay and death. The way of salvation is to escape from this flux of phenomena, to the motionless, timeless centre of the wheel, where all is peace. Only there can one observe the movement, without being involved in it. The events of history are appearance, not reality. Whether the Buddha actually taught what is recorded or whether Jesus even lived is relatively unimportant—they are just different spokes by which one may escape to the still centre of the turning wheel.

On the other side, are the religions which see life as a road. History is a journey, a pilgrimage. Life is movement towards a goal. We do not know fully what that goal will be, but God has revealed himself in the events of human history, enough for us to know the way. The glorious goal ahead gives meaning and inspiration to our daily life, so we can rejoice even in our tribulations.

To be sure, this is a vast over-simplification. The religions elaborate these images with great subtlety and with much interaction. But it is broadly true that Buddhism and Hinduism are religions of the wheel, of an escape from the illusions of history; while Judaism, Christianity and Islam are religions of the road, finding life's meaning in a future consummation of human history. (We might add Marxist Communism to the 'religions of the road'. African traditional religion stands interestingly with a foot in both camps— without an ultimate goal in view, yet finding meaning and purpose in the history of the tribe and the events of family life.)

Let us take a closer look at the 'religions of the road', Judaism, Christianity and Islam. Are these more or less the same? Here we have a common belief in One God, who created and sustains the world. Through the events of history and through prophecy, God reveals his mercy and judgement, and calls man to obedience. All three religions find their origin in Abraham, and tell of his descendants, Isaac and Ishmael, Moses and David.

Yet again we find striking diversity. Of Judaism we must speak with special tenderness, in view of the sufferings that 'Christendom' has inflicted on the children of Israel. But while Judaism certainly does not refuse to receive converts, it has remained basically the religion for people of a common descent, and not a religion for all peoples. Of Islam too we must speak gently, in view of the tensions of Pakistan and the

Near East. But we see in Islam a kind of theocracy or more exactly, 'nomocracy'. Islam attempts to fulfil God's will by the formation of a community where every detail of ritual, personal relationships, business affairs and even government will be ruled by divinely inspired law. These, we must say, are very different conceptions from the Christian ideal of a fellowship in Christ, led by the Holy Spirit.

When we come to the person of Jesus Christ, the divergence is acute. Jesus' ethical teaching has obvious roots in the Old Testament, so that the Jew easily respects it. A Jewish scholar, Klausner, has given us one of the most sensitive studies of Jesus' teaching. Yet for Judaism, Jesus' claim to be the Messiah and Son of God remains a blasphemy, or at best a tragic misunderstanding.

Islam seems at first closer to Christianity. 'We do believe in Jesus,' say many Muslims, 'so why won't you believe in Muhammad?' The Qur'an gives to Jesus the titles of Messiah, Prophet and Messenger of God. It relates his birth to the Virgin Mary, his healing of the blind and the lepers, and his raising of the dead. Muslims widely believe in a 'second coming' of Jesus at the last day. Muhammad believed himself to be following in Jesus' footsteps. Yet after all, for Islam, Jesus is no more than a created being, a prophet only to the children of Israel, not Lord and Saviour of the world. Islam denies that Jesus called himself Son of God, or taught his disciples to call themselves sons of God. Most poignantly, Islam denies that Jesus died on the Cross—for surely God would have protected so great a prophet from such a shameful defeat!

4—ATG * *

'We would like to agree with you', say some Muslims. 'So please leave out those differences, and let us just agree on one God and Jesus as his Messenger.' We appreciate the good intentions of the proposal, but we cannot compromise. Christians believe in God, above all, *as he revealed himself in Jesus Christ*. Central to our belief is that 'Christ died for our sins. . . he was buried, and raised to life the third day', and 'God has made him both Lord and Christ.'

This brief survey of religions is not by any means to be taken as a refutation; it is not intended as an easy 'proof' that they are wrong and Christianity is right. The point is that they are quite evidently different in their teaching. Indeed people of other religions will not be grateful to us for ignoring their individuality. To take just one more example: a modern Hindu teacher claims it as one of the glories of Hinduism that it has the 'courage' (which Christianity lacks) to worship the evil principle of the universe as well as the good. Here is a belief simply incompatible with the Christian's faith in the God and Father of our Lord Jesus Christ.

It was originally planned for this chapter to be called 'the uniqueness of the Gospel'. The Gospel *is* unique, but it did not seem particularly significant to say so, when each one of the great religions has its own uniqueness. What is much more in question is *the universality of the Gospel*. Do we dare to say that, out of all these different faiths, it is the Gospel of Jesus Christ which the whole world needs to hear and believe? We must look more closely at the Gospel's claim to be universal.

The Old Testament, scripture for Jews and Christians alike, opens with God's creation of the universe, the fall of man, the flood and God's covenant with 'every living creature'. Then the story narrows to Abraham and his descendants, and narrows again to the small tribe which God delivered from slavery in Egypt and to whom he entrusted his law. Ex 12:37 tells us that this chosen people consisted of a mere six thousand men. Yet there is universal significance in God's dealings with this little band. In Abraham's seed all the families of the earth are to find blessing. God is Lord of the whole earth, and Israel is a 'Kingdom of priests', chosen so that through them all nations may know the Lord and see his glory. Repeatedly the children of Israel disobey or forget their calling and come under judgement; but God's plan is undefeated. He will raise up a purified remnant; a new rod from the stem of Jesse; a servant to be a light to the nations, and who will suffer and die to bear the sins not of a chosen few, but of the many (Gen 12:1-3; Ex 19:6; Is 2:1-4; 11:1 ff; 49:5-6; 53:12).

Into this universalist tradition came Jesus, believing himself to be the fulfilment of Jewish prophecy. The prophets had pictured a 'day of the Lord', when God's rule would be manifested; the eyes of the blind would be opened, the ears of the deaf unstopped; the lame would leap as a hart and good tidings would be preached to the poor, afflicted ones. 'Are you he who is to come?' asked John the Baptist. 'Go and tell John the signs you have seen and heard', replied Jesus. 'If by the finger of God I cast out demons, then be sure that the Kingdom of God has already come upon you' (Is 35:5 f; 61:5 f; Luke 7:18-23, 11:20).

Our Muslim friends sometimes embarrass us by recalling the sayings of Jesus: 'Go nowhere among the Gentiles, and enter no town of the Samaritans, but go rather to the lost sheep of the house of Israel', and 'I was sent only to the lost sheep of the house of Israel' (Matt 10:5-6; 15:24).

Did Jesus deny his own universal mission? Two comments may be made here. First, the sayings must be understood in their contexts. Matthew 10 refers to the *first* occasion on which Jesus sent his disciples out to preach. On this particular occasion he limited their mission to the house of Israel, but later he did try to go with them to the Samaritans (Luke 9:51-5). In Matthew 15, Jesus' words must be understood as a test of the Gentile woman's faith. Note well that he ended by praising her faith and healing her daughter.

Our second comment is perhaps the more important. It is precisely in accordance with the universalist tradition of the Old Testament that Jesus should preach first to the house of Israel, and call out from them the disciples who should declare God's salvation to the end of the earth. So Jesus gives his life a ransom for many, he rises victorious from the dead, the Spirit is to be poured out on all mankind. It is Matthew's Gospel (in contrast to 10:6 and 15:24, above) which now reports the universal rule of Jesus and the universal mission of his disciples: 'All authority in heaven and on earth has been given to me. Go therefore, and make disciples of all nations.'

But what about those who are already good religious men, worshippers of the one God? Do they need to be made disciples of Jesus Christ? Yes, it was just to such men, devout Jewish pilgrims, that the Apostles preached on the day of Pentecost. 'Repent and be baptized every one of you in the name of Jesus Christ for the forgiveness of your sins'; and later, to the religious leaders, 'there is no other name under heaven given among men, by which we must be saved' (Ac 2:38; 4:12).

We come again, as promised above, to the text, Ac 10:34-35: 'God treats all men alike. Whoever fears him and does what is right, is acceptable to him, no matter what race he belongs to.' This text teaches us to discern the work of God in men who have not yet known Jesus Christ. How indeed could any man come to know Christ, except that God first draws him? But the text has sometimes been misapplied to suggest that, as the god-fearing non-Christian is already acceptable to God, there is no more need for him to hear the Gospel. The context teaches quite the opposite. God accepts Cornelius's prayers and works of charity—and for that very reason sends Simon Peter with the Gospel and pours out the Holy Spirit on this Gentile household.

The epistles elaborate the universality of Christ. In him everything was created and all things hold together. In him all the fullness of God was pleased to dwell. Through him God chose to reconcile all things whether on earth or in heaven. At his name every knee should bow and every tongue confess that Jesus Christ is Lord, to the glory of God the Father. In the end he will abolish every evil power, and so deliver up the Kingdom to God the Father. (Col 1:16-20; Phil 2:9-12; 1 Cor 15:24 f)

The goal is before us, not just our personal enjoyment of salvation, but the summing up of all things in Christ. The history of Israel and of Christ shows us the road; Christ himself is the Way; we travel hopefully, often bewildered, yet sure by faith that we shall arrive!

The Gospel, then, claims to be universal. It claims to be the truth for all men and for all time. You can believe it or reject it; don't try to water it down to something local and temporary.

But (to repeat) do we dare to believe it? Just look at the Church:

> *Though with a scornful wonder*
> *Men see her sore oppressed,*
> *By schisms rent asunder,*
> *By heresies distressed ...*

But probably hardest to explain away is the sheer undistinguished ordinariness of so much church life. The average Christian seems often no better or worse than his non-Christian contemporary. Like the people of other religions we pray individually and together, we read and treasure our sacred scriptures, we try to live up to ethical ideals—it is not at once obvious that there is any radical difference between their religious life and ours.

Some Christian thinkers have tried to solve this problem by making a sharp distinction between 'the Gospel' and 'the religions'. 'The Gospel' is the essential revelation in Christ, the message of God's judgement and mercy. 'The religions' are what men do by way of worship, belief and practice. Certainly then, there is a Christian religion or 'Christianity', a tradition of religious practices which has many points of contact with other religions. Like them, it is full of human frailty. Just like them, it stands under the judgement of God. No absolute truth or universality can be claimed for 'Christianity'. But (so this theory goes) we claim universality for 'the Gospel', God's word to all mankind.

This distinction has been helpful, in emphasising that the Gospel is no mere development or fulfilment of other religions; that the convert to Christ must make in some ways a radical break with his past. But in the end it seems that the distinction is artificial. God knows what 'the Gospel' is in itself, apart from religious practice. But *we* can know the Gospel only as it is believed, practised and preached by Christians, only as it is incarnated in the Church. We cannot finally separate the Gospel from the Church, in all its weakness. We must still ask, what has the Church got, that enables us to believe in the universality of the Gospel?

Others in this book will write in detail about the Gospel in the Bible, and its expression today. Here we can offer only a brief answer: that the special characteristic of the Church (when it is at all faithful to the Gospel) is a profound distrust of religiousness.*

This is a paradox. The Christian cannot avoid being religious. Yet it is not there that he finds his security. On at least two occasions Jesus was asked, 'What shall I do to inherit eternal life?' Once he answered with the story of the Good Samaritan, in which the two religious figures are plainly on the way to perdition, while the non-religious Samaritan is in the way of truth. On the other occasion, Jesus said to the rich young ruler (I paraphrase), 'You're already observing all the religious rules, but still you haven't found peace? Sell all you have and give to the poor' (Luke 10:25 ff; 18:18 f; cf. Luke 18:9 f).

At the heart of Christian faith is the record of Jesus' struggle with the Pharisees. Those most earnest and devout religious men, with scripture at their fingertips, were precisely the ones who rejected God's light in Christ. 'Harlots and publicans' could enter the Kingdom of heaven before them. So Christians are painfully aware that religiousness is no guarantee of salvation, but is often the very source of self-righteousness and spiritual blindness. Our religion can be the idol which we worship instead of God!

Hence we cannot believe in the universality of Christian religiousness. We are not trying to persuade

* By 'religiousness' I mean devotion to the outward practices of religion: hymns, prayers, creeds and sermons; being a bishop or a parson, a society steward or a trustee; burning incense or shouting hallelujah; building churches or giving to charity. All of these can be glorious expressions of faith—or they can be works of self-righteousness; all can be marks of sanctity—or of sanctimoniousness.

Hindus or Muslims to change over to our forms of religious practice. Even if we tried, we should be unlikely to have much success.

But we live in a world where fixed religious practice seems to be growing less important. Life is being *secularized* even for religious believers. Many Christians fear this process, as a threat to our faith. But other Christians believe that this is the greatest opportunity for the Gospel to be heard and understood all round the world. They say the Gospel is itself a 'secular announcement'—not a set of ready-made doctrines and rituals to be swallowed whole—but a word from God about forgiveness and reconciliation, about responsible use of our freedom, about war and peace, love and hate, justice and mercy—the very problems to which secularized man is seeking an answer.

Then the Gospel is what all men everywhere need. And if the Church, however feebly, has been hearing and believing God's word in Christ, and experiencing some answer to these problems, it could be poised as never before to demonstrate the universal relevance of the Gospel.

A last word, on the practical approach to men of other faiths. Some Christians have made fine efforts of understanding, but much too often there is a sad history of Christian prejudice and aggressiveness. The most important thing for us is to rediscover Christ's command, 'Love thy neighbour as thyself.' Let the Church really be a fellowship of people who love one another, and radiate their love to all around.

Then we need to be clear what is the Gospel to which we bear witness. Too often we have made the impression of coming as a rival religion, with a fixed ritual and doctrine, arguing to prove that 'we are right and you are wrong'. Doctrine and creed are valuable in the life of the Church. But probably in our witness to men of other faiths, we should first emphasize the events of history in which we discern God's revelation—supremely what Christ did, said and suffered; and then testify to the meaning which faith in Christ has for us in our personal and communal living.

Even before we try to give any witness, we shall do well first to listen, trying sincerely to understand without prejudgement the faith which is precious to our non-Christian friend. This is in any case the way of love. But also by understanding the other's faith, we shall be able to explain our own more intelligibly.

Inevitably we shall long and pray for our partners to find Christ and join our fellowship; yet we shall be meticulous to respect their spiritual freedom, and patient to leave the issues with God.

In many parts of Africa a frank Muslim-Christian dialogue takes place spontaneously, at various social and educational levels. 'Islam in Africa Project' has a dozen workers in different parts of Africa, helping the Christians 'to understand Islam and the Muslim, in view of the Church's task of faithfully interpreting the Gospel of Christ'. At a Study Centre in Nigeria Christian pastors, from many churches in many lands, enthusiastically learn to read and interpret at least a few verses of the Arabic Qur'an. Many

Muslims have been deeply appreciative of our little effort to understand them better.

In Britain, by and large the Church has yet to wake up to the presence in our midst of a quarter of a million Muslims, still more Sikhs, and not a few Hindus. What will it mean, to love these neighbours as ourselves? First, no doubt, it will mean a generous concern for their welfare and for a solution to race problems. We shall be specially sensitive to their fears as religious minorities. Then perhaps some readers of this book will study one of the religions, so that when the opportunity comes a genuine dialogue may occur. Perhaps you will find your own faith deepened and your sermons enlivened, from having reached out to understand the faith of others.

BOOKS

Christian Faith and Other Faiths—Stephen Neill (Oxford University Press)
The Finality of Faith—Lesslie Newbigin (SCM Press)
For statistics of Christian expansion, see Barrett, 'A.D. 2000: 350 million Christians in Africa' in *International Review of Missions,* January 1970

Communicating the Gospel

Eric W. Blennerhassett

1 But How?

We are appointed to be preachers of the Gospel at a time when our appointments take us to emptying churches, when preaching is at a discount, and when the Gospel is not what people seem to want to hear. Quite clearly, we have our problems.

What's gone wrong? I have heard preachers blame it on a number of things. Materialism. The younger generation. The secular age. The permissive society. The I'm-all-right-Jack, couldn't care less attitude. From their enjoyment of this kind of flagellation, I should guess that these are chiefly the sadists among us, extrovert in type, loud in voice, and increasingly irrelevant to all except themselves. Others have had a whale of a time bewailing (if you will pardon the expression) the failure of the church, the hypocrisy of Christians, and the irrelevance of our faith. But these, I guess, are the masochists among us, whose deliberately subdued voices and measured tones combine strangely with a steely glint in the eye, and who will be disappointed if they are not martyred by somebody before they are very much older. Me, I am a sado-masochist, and I have just been enjoying myself doing a bit of both.

What is to be done? Invent new orders of service? Have more guitars and less organ? Become better theologians, better speakers, better preachers? Or dig our heels in, fill our minds with noble thoughts about righteous remnants and the historic church, and go on in the old ways even if it means preaching to rows of wood and walls of brick? Maybe none of these things will do. Maybe we need a bit of each. But I for one find all these questions unanswerable at this level. When we have churches to run and appointments to fulfil, they may seem indeed to be the pressing questions. But I have no faith in finding piecemeal answers—at least, not without unearthing clearer aims and better reasons than we have touched upon so far.

If you get bogged down, move to higher ground where you can see more of the way things are—and perhaps discover a different approach. This, at any rate, is the only hope of a way through for me. I invite you to take the journey with me—but with one clear warning. I have a profound mistrust—which I expect you share—of people who write or speak on 'How to . . .' do this or that. If they really knew, they would be too busy doing it. This article is not going to be an exercise in getting coals to Newcastle. There will be no neat and tidy solutions, because I have none to offer. It will be instead an exploration. And if it does bring us back to where we started, I hope we shall have experienced something worth while on the way.

Part of the reason for getting bogged down is the loss of bearings, leading to a misreading of the situation. So when established institutions or ways of doing things break down, we blame the times we are living in, or the people, or the institutions, or ourselves. The blame may or may not be deserved; it certainly yields no solutions.

It is my belief that Christian communication is now in a state of breakdown. That if the church has failed, it is not because of lack of effort on our part, but because we have not been reading the signs of the times. That if the church and its message is being rejected by many because they do not care, it is also being rejected by many more because they do. But more than all these, I believe the chief reason for the breakdown is that we are now living at a crucial moment in the history of the world. It is a great melting-pot period of the kind that—until now—has only happened once in every four or five hundred years. New discoveries are being made. New powers are being released. New situations are confronting us. The old bottles are bursting because the wine is new.

At such a time we have to begin by questioning the assumptions that have grown up over the years. We are preachers of the Word. But what does that suggest about us? That we are good at talking for long periods in public? That we can deliver sermons of at least twenty minutes in length, because no man can do justice to the Gospel in less? That we can pray with unquenchable spontaneity because that proves it is the Holy Spirit and not our own commonsense? That we can give other people the impression of being closer to God than they are—for their encouragement, of course, and to the greater glory of God? And what does this suggest about the Word? That it is a set of doctrines that we are to teach? A sequence of words that has to be repeated? The printed page of the Holy Bible which we must read in lessons and expound in sermons? A kind of spiritual language which is specially suited to the pulpit? A religious vocabulary that we become adept at using for blessings, curses, and spiritual uplift? Saving truths to be uttered in given ways and in a certain order? Hidden secrets? Kerygma for the initiated? The full Gospel for the uninitiated? Endless yakity-yak?

So much for the bog. The point of preaching is that we should communicate. The point of communication is that meaning should pass from one to the other. If we do not make sense to others, we are not communicating. In which case, whether we call it preaching or not is immaterial; it has in fact become a nonsense. So where can we find a way through?

2 The Word That is Never Just Speech

We do not become preachers of the Gospel by repeating so-called Gospel words and phrases. We preach the Gospel only when we convey Gospel meanings to others. The Word that we are to communicate is something more than just speech.

111

God said, 'Let there be light', and there was light, according to the writer of Genesis. By which he was not describing a process, but communicating a faith. And the faith which he was communicating was something more than just a statement that God created all things. When a word is spoken it conveys meaning. So the Word of God is dramatically portrayed here as having creative power and meaning. It gives existence to meaning, and meaning to existence. We all have meaning, this man cries, because there is meaning at the heart of creation. The Word that gives us life gives us meaning too.

This is the understanding of the Word which Isaiah and all the prophets shared. For them, it was the source of meaning, and value and purpose. And when it was expressed, it clothed itself in a form which went out and became active in conveying that meaning, expressing that value, and bringing that creative purpose about. This, for John and the first Christians, is the Word that became flesh. And here is crystallized for us the Christian understanding of communication and of the Gospel.

But how did this come about? What was the experience that gave rise to this understanding? The answer is given us by the Gospel writers, as by the writers of Genesis and by the prophets, in dramatic form. Men first found themselves confronted in their ordinary workaday lives by Jesus, the son of a joiner from Nazareth. Their meeting with him had a certain quality of mutual recognition about it. However unlikely their circumstances, however unsatisfactory their situations, he acted as if he understood. They found with him a kind of acceptance which was warm and welcoming. This swiftly crystallized into an invitation which, though no less warm, was also demanding. At which point, those whose hearts were really set on other priorities turned down the invitation. Some did so politely and with regret, not understanding that this was a situation from which there could be no opting out; without knowing it, they were playing their part in his rejection. Others accepted, and instantly found themselves engaged in following him. They also found themselves thrown together in sharing the secrets of his nature and the crises of his life. From this there radiated from him to them, from them to him, and from them to each other, a new kind of loving which found its climax in the giving of his life for them all. This apparent defeat they found to be victory. This kind of loving was also an overcoming. And from that time on their business was to communicate this life and this love.

The turning point in this drama came with Jesus' question: 'Who do you say that I am?' And Peter answered: 'You are the Christ.' This is the Word of faith. The Word is not commandments. Not ethics. Not doctrines. Not even the stories of Jesus. The Word is an utterance of meaning, of value, of fulfillment. The Word is Christ.

Coming as we do after the event, we can easily slip into thinking of Christ as Jesus' surname. But it was not that at all. Jesus of Nazareth was the man whom they met and followed. Christ was the name they gave him when they wanted to express his value for them. God was in Christ, reconciling them to himself and to each other; they were to become the body of Christ, communicating his life through theirs. The Word had become flesh because there was no other way through. Not just Jesus' flesh. But their flesh. Our flesh. And there still is no other way through.

3 The Image That is Never Quite the Reality

If Peter was the first to respond to Jesus as the Christ, it was not a significance thought up by Peter and imposed by him on the man from Nazareth; it was a discovery by him of the meaning that Jesus was communicating. From the pleasure that Jesus expressed, it is clear that he regarded this as a moment of truth, and a breakthrough for his communication. We could say therefore that Jesus was the first communicator of Christ, of the new life that was God-centred and man-expressed. This is not to imply that there was any division between Jesus and the Christ. What it does imply is that the communication of Christ by Jesus required a self-knowledge on his part, a fearlessness in bringing to the surface what he found, and an imaginativeness in sharing this meaning from the depths of his being to the depths of the being of others.

Jesus' task as communicator was to find the form which would fit the meaning in each situation. As he did so, he became necessarily involved in further explorations of the meaning. This is what took him from his experience at Jordan into the wilderness, to explore the meaning which he was to clothe in the forms of his Galilean ministry; or from the experience of that ministry up to the mountain-top, before he set his face towards Jerusalem; or from the city and the last supper into Gethsemane garden, before he went to the final show-down. So meaning and form interacted upon each other in highly mobile patterns of communication.

The forms which he chose were those which could appeal to the imaginations of his contemporaries, and point beyond themselves to the meanings he had to convey. In so doing he gave fresh significance to imagery. His choice of images had a three-way overlap. They overlapped with some familiar situation. They overlapped with the one aspect of the meaning he wished to communicate. And they overlapped with the attitudes and desires of the people he addressed.

His verbal imagery operated at many levels. The shortest and sharpest was the direct metaphor. 'Go and tell that fox . . .' he said of King Herod, giving in two words a vivid assessment of the king's untrustworthiness and cruelty. 'You whitewashed sepulchres, respectable on the outside, but inside full of dead men's bones', was his description of the Pharisees, in which form was fitted to meaning with devastating effect. According to John, he also used this kind of imagery of himself. 'I am the vine . . .' 'I am the good shepherd . . .' 'I am the light of the world . . .'

In getting across the theme of the kingdom, he used a multiplication of extended metaphors which he introduced with some such question as: 'What is the kingdom of heaven like? With what shall I compare it?' Then followed images of hidden treasure, a costly pearl, a lost coin, seed growing secretly, and many more, each set in the shortest imaginable story of what happened when. . . . The treatment is dramatic, the interest is in the action, and the climax provides the clue to the meaning. Likewise with his longer stories—the longest of which were still short by our standards—such as the sower, the prodigal son, and the good Samaritan. In all these cases his hearers were drawn into a dramatic situation, given a clue in the twist of events, and asked to make their own discoveries and judgements. Every time the image is made to point, however quizzically, beyond itself for completion. It quickens the awareness that ultimately every man must make his own discoveries, decide his own loyalties, give his own love.

4 The Action That is Never Fully Completed

But Jesus did not leave it there. So fully did he integrate the expressive form with the hidden meaning that his actions became part of the imagery on yet another level. The images of action that he rejected are as significant as the ones that he accepted. He refused the roles of wonder-worker, political power-seeker, military revolutionary, nationalistic messiah. He accepted instead the roles of communicator, healer, leader, liberator. Every act made sense within each situation because he began at the points of greatest need—whether in talking to the people, healing the sick, developing the new community, or throwing down his challenges to the leaders of church and state. Yet every act also pointed beyond itself, because it expressed something more of the meanings that were his to communicate. This is seen most clearly of all as the climax approaches—in his approach to Jerusalem as the envoy of peace sitting on an ass; in his acting out of the role of Isaiah's suffering servant; in his identification with Passover pilgrim, priest, and, finally, sacrifice.

'It is finished', he cried. In so doing he expressed the acceptance of limitation that is one of the hallmarks— and I do not say this lightly—of every great communicator. He had done all he could at that moment and in that situation. No man has greater love than this. In one sense this was the full Gospel which was once for all, and to that extent it was finished. Not even he could give more or add further meaning if he came back and repeated it all a thousand times.

But in another sense the Gospel is still being played out. Every situation cries out now for someone to act out the meaning of Christ from within it. And in every life there are moments which cry out for a dying to self and a resurrection in and for the other.

The active imagery of Jesus not only pointed beyond itself. It constituted his commission. And this commission he passed on to his followers. It was in acting out his meaning that they were to celebrate his presence. Their action would become his, and his action would become theirs. Which commission to go and do likewise he now passes on to us.

5 The Body That We Are on the Way to Becoming

Paul told his fellow Christians that they were the body of Christ. As anyone can tell from the trouble that he had with them—and that they had with each other—

this was anything but an accurate description. But this was the communication of a prophetic word, in that it was their true vocation, and the utterance of it played a powerful part towards bringing about its fulfilment. It was a word—or metaphor or image—which sprang out of the life which the disciples shared with Jesus and communicated to others. Like them, we are now both the receivers and communicators of this life.

Christ is not the surname of Jesus. It is the name of the body that we are becoming. This happens with us as with the first disciples. As we enter into the secrets of his nature and say yes, this is recognizably ourselves as we were born to be. As we become involved in the crises of his life and say yes, this is the nature of our job in the world. As we learn how to share with him and with each other and say yes, this is the way of real communication.

Our nature is such that in the usual way only the top tenth shows, as with the iceberg. This is the level on which we normally communicate. But the most interesting part of us—and the most important too—is the submerged nine-tenths. Every creative artist knows this, and it is one of the most demanding parts of his vocation to undergo successive acts of self-knowledge. His exploration will take him, as far as he is able, down through every level of his being. It takes a kind of courage which can be developed as it is acted upon. Then with equal courage he must bring to the surface what he finds—often to his own surprise. And then, because he is committed to the business of communication, he must shape his discoveries into some com-

municable form. At which point others will be drawn
in through the sharing that he offers. And when a
moment of truth takes place, the curious thing about it
is that while it springs from his readiness to reveal,
what they experience is a revelation of themselves.
The awareness which they share comes as an awareness of a reality which is common to them all. Where
two or three are gathered together. . . .

It is a paradox of communication that the more
deeply personal it is, the more widespread is likely to
be its appeal. This is because beneath the distinctions
and differences we share a common human nature.
The cost of such communication is self-giving. Which
is what Christ is about. The Gospel which Jesus communicated was not a message. What he communicated was Christ. The Gospel was himself. To share
at depth, and every other level, is to love like Christ.
This is how he shares himself with us. And in sharing
with him and with each other we are on the way to
becoming the body of Christ.

6 Action Together At Points of Need

Just as modern communications cut across all boun-
daries and criss-cross all areas of knowledge and experience, so must we in the communications we offer
and receive. Our starting point, like that of Jesus, is
to be found at the points of need. But these cannot be
discovered thoroughly or met effectively without the
partnership of all concerned.

There are the basic wants of people—in vastly
greater numbers than we care to think—which

contrast hideously with the squandering of wealth by the increasingly affluent. Hunger that kills human life. Homelessness that destroys human respect. There are the needs of people in their individuality. Suffering and death are always with us, but are no less important in the drama of human life for that. And when suffering includes drugs, alcoholism, and nervous breakdowns, and when death includes loneliness and suicide, we have much to discover and meet. There are the needs of people in their relationships. Neither sex nor race can be regarded as new on the human scene. But new freedoms in sex and new re-alignments in race confront us with issues which go right to the heart of our faith. There are the needs of people for equal human rights, whatever their colour, race or religion. Fairer justice for every man—and I do not mean only in the courts—and greater freedom for every man are not just nice thoughts or impossible ideals; they need to be championed now more urgently than ever before. And since one of the characteristics of this age is the amassing of new power, we have to ask whether Christian faith and humility have now to be related in quite new ways to the exercise of that power—scientific, economic, political, and environmental.

It may be that not much is achieved by speaking of our needs in shopping-list terms like that. But I have done so to indicate some of the things about which we need to remind each other constantly. And to indicate by the limitations of such a list that these needs in other ways, and other needs of quite different kinds, have still to be uncovered and met in each and every local situation.

When so many of the ancient barriers are being thrown down, it is surely not our task to run the churches, or order the services, or organize the activities, for the sake of the church. That could only bring about poor results, and divisive consequences. Our task now is to be the church in the community— communicating at the points of need and responsibility; in partnership with all who care for and serve in the community; for the sake of the people in it, with the best possible results, and reconciling consequences. The Word-become-flesh must dwell among us in every part of the community if we are to catch glimpses of his glory.

7 Imaginative Explorations of Imagery

To explore the work of Jesus as communicator is to encounter an imagination which is free-ranging in its activity and powerful in its impact. So it is in varying degrees with every effective communicator. Perhaps there is no quality which we need to develop more at this melting-pot time than our imagination. It has been stifled for too long in Christian communication. Now that imagination is finding new freedoms in every other field of endeavour, we simply must give it new freedom in the ways in which we believe, and act on our beliefs, and give expression to them in worship.

As the derivation of the word suggests, our imagination works chiefly through imagery. Finding the form for each situation is now very much our business. With, I suggest, the test of the threefold overlap to help us in our search—that it should overlap with things or processes which are familiar in our daily life, and with the meanings for faith to be conveyed, and with the interests and feelings that are real to us now. And if our imagination is given its proper freedom, it will not allow us to stick these elements together in artificial fashion in order to bear out a statement or prove a point already decided. It will make possible instead the discovery of something that will lead us to fresh and often surprising results.

It may be that shepherd and potter and sower now suggest a way of life that has gone for ever. But the principle of exploring our present occupations and methods and technologies for their relevance to our developing life is as valid now as ever it was. If we use the imagery of outmoded occupations because they still have appeal to our psyche and because they are vividly suggestive of meaning, we shall be aware that they are weak on familiarity; some extra work on presentation will be needed at this point. With contemporary occupations on the other hand, familiarity may be strong and appeal may be immediate, but meaning for faith is likely to be weak; some extra work on throwing out clues will be needed here.

The same is true of topographical features and social life. Rock, spring, river, mountain, tree; family, household, city, kingdom, have their strengths and weaknesses which may be clarified by this three-way test. And so also with clover-leaf, switchboard, computer, crane, airport, control

tower, escalator, underground, railway station, community, council, parliament, television, radio, cinema,
theatre, teach-in, love-in, pop show, and so on.

Most universal of the images are those which are
essential to human life. Like the elements of earth,
air, fire, and water. Like food and drink. Like love
and hate.

If we carry out our search for new forms here instead of with what we have always done the way we
have always done it, we can press home the question;
what new and imaginative uses can we make of
imagery now? In words? In action? In exploration
together? In celebration together? With fire, and
water, and bread, and wine? In church? In homes?
In factories? In council chambers? In streets? I
believe that what we shall discover will be not a new
set of sermon illustrations, but new kinds of communication and new meanings for life. And that not
by accident, but because the Word that dwells
amongst us is the presence of Christ.

8 Speech Which Participates in the Word

So we come back full circle to the words that give
meaning. We can perhaps now see that speech is
itself another form of imagery. By itself it is simply
noises that we make with our voices, or patterns that
we put on paper. It is not itself the reality. If only we
had understood this more clearly and more often, we
should all have been saved a lot of grief.

One of the greatest dangers in communication is
the tendency to identify the reality, or our under-

standing of it, with the images or speech through
which we try to communicate it. The ancient prohib-
ition of idolatry suggests some early understanding of
these dangers, though the reasons were expressed in
different terms from ours. If in this unsuperstitious
age we are in little danger from graven images, we
cannot say the same for idolatry of the verbal sort.

We tend to identify all too easily the Christian
faith with the doctrines through which we express it.
Or the Gospel with certain words or phrases as if
fixed for all time. Or God with the three-letter
word—or any other label that we try to stick on him.
Once this happens, disastrous things inevitably follow. Like building church structures and habits of
religious observance around the form rather than the
meaning. Like a transference of loyalty from the
spirit to the letter. Like a reversal of the religious
relationship, making us users of religion and God,
and putting us firmly in charge. Like an insistence on
superficial conformity rather than on love in action.
All of which leads to bigotry, division, and all un-
charitableness.

As with all good imagery, speech is not the reality,
but its work is to express its meaning and evoke some
response to it. To be effective it should overlap with
some familiar feature of our shared experience, with
the meaning to be communicated, and with the
feelings and longings that are for real at the
present time.

Because for us the Word is Christ, for our speech
in Christian communication we might take our clues
from him. We should then try to make it descriptive

and dramatic rather than exhortatory and prosy; personal rather than impersonal; active rather than passive; indicative rather than subjunctive; concrete rather than abstract; particular rather than general. With maximum economy of time and verbiage, it should be just sufficient to make its impact—and no more. Its presentation and placing in, say, an order of service should be determined by these ends, and not by verbal superstition or habit. It should involve the listener in a situation of awareness, of choice, and of resolution. And it should point beyond itself for completion in Christ. That way, our words may become indications of the Word in which they participate.

9 A Matter of Life and Death

It may seem that if we slip from the moorings of established institutions, traditional services, accustomed actions, and familiar phraseology, we will be in danger of losing the urgency of Christian communication and the distinctiveness of the Gospel. But none of these things constitute the reality that we are to communicate, and insofar as they obscure it, we should welcome their death as a happy release.

The church is no longer the chief medium of communication—even of the Gospel. It is no longer the local cultural community, or the social service organisation, or the entertainment and leisure centre that once it was. It is not even the structural spiritual authority for dictating the faith, enforcing the morality, and exerting the discipline which the world requires. It is perhaps learning that to save its life is to lose it; readiness to lose it for Christ's sake is the way to find it.

What then of the communication of the Gospel now and in the future? It seems to me that far from destroying its urgency and diminishing its distinctiveness, our exploration emphasizes both. I believe the communication of the Gospel to be a matter of life and death—now more than ever. As to the question how, we still cannot offer neat and tidy answers. But I believe we are being given several clear pointers: towards worship which is more flexible in its order, more varied in its timing, locations and emphases, more multi-dimensional in its use of all the talents, and more participational for all involved in it; towards Christian advocacy which is exercised more in the community, in mixed groups, in house fellowships, and less confined to church circles; towards service which is carried out more with others who care for the community at the points of need and responsibility; towards spelling out in as many different ways as possible the message that 'You are the body of Christ'. Not just to the church. But to the community and the world.

I believe that for this kind of communication to be carried out in the community, the office of local preacher as such will be seen to be irrelevant. The priesthood of all believers was a Protestant concept. The worker priest was a Catholic concept. Both have failed through misunderstanding and half measures. Could we not now try again by bringing both together in a new form of ministry? Not only by finding 'secular' work for the ordained, but also by finding an ordination for 'secular' workers? With a new name that would suggest much more than the delivery of twenty-minute sermons at 11.00 and 6.30 on Sundays in church? A name that would suggest much richer and more varied forms of communication? A name better suited to expressing the vocation of the community—to become the body of Christ?